Daughters
Praising, Speaking Up, Talking Back

In Search Of
Fatherhood

Stories From Women Around The World

Kevin Renner

This book is dedicated to Katherine and Julia.
You taught me what it means to loves and filled my heart with joy.

When you came into this world
Needing to be held
I was waiting to be with you.

When you were a little girl
And I was your daddy
I found my bliss being with you.

When you are a teenager
And I do not matter much
I will be with you.

When you are intoxicated with your first love
And heartbroken when it ends
I will be with you.

When you are a young adult
And find your anger toward me
I will be with you.

When you are in middle age
And we become friends
I will be with you.

When you are in old age
And I have passed
I will be with you.

When you take your last breath
And depart from this world
I will be with you.

CONTENTS

Preface

"I want my daddy back!"

I remember this scene as if it were yesterday. My oldest daughter Julia was two.

We were vacationing with another couple. I had a back injury and couldn't lift her. So my friend Brian held her, a few feet away from me, and she didn't like that. She wanted *her* daddy back, not some other girl's. And she let everyone know.

In the course of writing this book I got to hear how strongly daughters want their fathers back. It's buried deeply for some; it's right at the surface for others. But you can't talk with 50 women who are baring their souls and not feel their longing for the fathers they wanted more of, or something different from.

Julia is fifteen now. Before she could walk, she used to crawl to our front door at about six o'clock every night and wait for me to get home from work. When she was four I took her for an overnight camping trip in the mountains. She woke up at five o'clock in the morning, sat up in our tent, and said, "Daddy, I'm cold." So I pulled her sleeping bag next to mine and hugged her as we both fell back asleep. When she was twelve, I got to watch her compete in The National Science Bowl for middle school students. The magical moments with her, and with her sister, have been abundant.

Katherine—or Kat as she's known—is four years younger. When she was almost two, Kat used to greet me at our front door as well when I arrived home from work. For some reason known only to her, she began licking my hand when I walked in. "What am I now," I asked one night, "your personal salt lick?" The next evening, and then for several months, she greeted me by running to the front door and shouting, "Salt lick!" and then licking my hand.

When she was four we invented a game called "Get Me." I'd sit on the living room floor, and she'd run circles around me yelling, "Get me, get me, get me!" Then I'd strike like a cobra and grab her with my arms or legs, wrestle her to the ground, and tickle her. A few years later, I made up "Fish Story," a bedtime tale about a small fish that befriends a leaf that fell on its mountain stream. They spend a lifetime together, migrating to the ocean, swimming to warmer water during the winter, then finding their way back three years later to the small stream where the story began. For months, I would lie down on Kat's bed with her, and tell her that story every night as she fell asleep.

Julia was in eighth grade and Kat was in fourth when I began this journey to understand daughterhood. As I began reflecting on how fathers shape their daughters, it struck me as odd that there are trainers, teachers, and coaches everywhere for everything—how to drive, get fit, write employee performance appraisals, learn software, play music, you name it. And over the course of our lives, men get instructed in dozens, if not hundreds, of areas—how to swim, camp, play baseball, drive, police the streets, manage a business, take care of patients. But who's training the world's dads on how to father their daughters? And do we have any more important job in our lives?

Just about anyone responsible for children faces training and certification requirements—teachers, therapists, doctors. Yet fathers can be utterly inept from their child's birth until their legal entry into adulthood. There are no requirements whatsoever for fatherhood, beyond the ability to fertilize an egg. Can't fruit flies do that?

This book includes stories from women whose fathers have been everything from heroic to horrific. All of the stories are authentic, and quotes are taken from recorded transcripts of conversations we had. In cases where women did not want their identities revealed, fictitious names were used, and those women appear by first name only.

When full first and last names are shown, these are the women's true identities. In most cases where a father's name is used, an assumed name has been created.

Also, many of the women spoke English as a secondary language. So in some of the interviews the English is broken. I did not correct this in my manuscript as I wanted to retain as much of the authenticity, rhythm, and poetic beauty of their voices as I could.

Introduction

Katie and I were young when we separated for good. Or so we thought. We were twelve. She was the first girl I kissed. One summer day before seventh grade, we were hanging out at an old shack in the woods between our homes. We called it the Sugar Shack, fittingly. It was the sweetest summer of my life.

My eleven-year-old brother Kurt was there along with a few other kids. We were playing the kissing game "Spin the Bottle," and I was hoping the bottle would point to Katie and me so we could make out. But when it did, I panicked. Time stood still. My brain froze. I couldn't move. Disgusted, Kurt looked at me—his older brother—and declared, "This is how you do it." Then he walked up to my sweetheart and kissed her like he was James Bond.

Humiliated, I walked over and kissed Katie too. My heart pounded, my face was flushed, and my body shook. In the same instant I experienced terror and bliss. It was the crescendo of my summer, yet may have been the beginning of the end for Katie and me. Junior high school started a month later. I was the dweeb—four feet ten, 87 pounds—with the cutest girlfriend in seventh grade. This was junior high school; there were real men to be had. Katie and I went our separate ways.

A few years later, I was living in California and getting my driver's license. Katie was in Oregon getting an abortion. Shortly after that,

I was studying at Berkeley and she was stripping in men's clubs. The arcs of our lives had touched and kissed for an innocent moment in time, just as the magical bloom of adolescence was beginning to open. And then the moment was gone.

I didn't truly know Katie until 40 years later. That's when I found her in Nevada, and asked if she would tell me her story for this book. It took a year for us to get together. When we did, I came to understand what happened as she was growing up, and how she tried to take her own life three times in later years. As well, I came face-to-face with the broken father inside of her.

Parenting is hard. Katie's father struggled with it, and most would say he failed, at least for the first 50 years of her life. I love being a dad, yet I certainly have struggled with it, too. I didn't start on this book because I was a parenting expert. Rather, like fathers everywhere, I had no idea what it means to be a girl in a relationship with her dad. Two years ago I realized how little I knew about raising daughters, and that there wasn't anything more important in my life. That disconnect troubled me. I began asking myself what I had left to teach my daughters. I wondered what they will long for as women that they didn't get from me.

My girls were nine and thirteen. How had that happened so fast? I realized I had been living in my private cocoon of work and stress, semi-conscious, on autopilot. At 52, I began a mid-life awakening. I was thirteen years into fatherhood, and felt like I was stumbling in the dark while my daughters had blown through childhood.

These questions and self-doubts hit me shortly after Christmas. I live in Portland, Oregon, and the entire area was buried under two feet of snow, an all-time record. This city gets paralyzed by two inches. Everything shut down. I couldn't go to work. For the first time in years, my agitated mind went still. I do mean agitated, too. I dreamed once that as I checked into a doctor's office I signed my name as "To Do" at the reception desk. But during this snowstorm, as my mind idled for the first time in years, my questions began about how fathers shape daughters, for better or worse.

I wanted to better understand what daughters absorb from their fathers and how that happens. I also felt that time was short for me. So I decided to explore fatherhood from a place I couldn't directly experience: The hearts and souls of grown-up daughters. I wanted women—for every one of them is a daughter—to teach me about fathering daughters.

I wanted to hear them reflect on what they had taken in from their fathers, and what they didn't get that they still yearned for. I wanted to find out about this special relationship, and how it set their lives on the trajectories that they'd traveled, so that I could do a better job with my own daughters.

I'm not a psychotherapist. I don't consider myself a writer. When I pitched a big-name book agent from L.A. with my idea for this work she asked, "Who are you?" I wanted to blurt back, "I'm nobody; I'm just another Dad. I'm Everyman. That's why this matters."

"I'll tell you what to do," she said. "You go interview Britney Spears and Lindsay Lohan...now that's what will sell."

Brilliant. The world waits with baited breath. Paris, anyone? Kim Kardashian?

This work is for my daughters, for me, for dads and daughters everywhere. This was something I simply felt compelled to do. So I began my journey in search of fatherhood.

Equipped with a recorder, I talked with women about their inner pain and joy, looking for lessons large and small. The women were rich and poor; well-known and anonymous; lesbian, straight, and transgender. They included a retired state Supreme Court judge, executives, and unemployed women. I spoke with professional athletes and former drug addicts. I met women with lives of abundance and others who had been homeless. They were from Liberia, Lithuania, Germany, China, North America, Holland, India, Mexico, Saudi Arabia, Iran, and places in between, seventeen countries in all, plus women who were native North American and Hawaiian Islander.

Their lives spanned seven decades, from their twenties through their eighties.

We talked for hours, until many of them couldn't talk any more. The conversations felt like taking the top off a volcano; the stories came up and out so naturally, and down their own paths like lava streams finding their way. And it's not just that the stories came up so naturally, it was *how* they did, as if they had a life and will of their own.

I quickly came to sense that the stories wanted to come out, to find their expression, to have someone hear them. That struck me most vividly as I sat in with a tow truck driver in her 80s, and listened as she shared her tears and pain that had been buried for 70 years. It occurred to me how deeply we all want to be heard, to be known for who we really are, to be understood, appreciated, and connected with.

I was struck by how intensely women feel the lasting influence of their fathers. I suspect that most men have no idea how deep those feelings run, or the strength and longevity of their impact. Nearly all of the women cried during our conversations. They helped me see and feel that, at its core, the father-daughter relationship is a universal love story of enormous depth. In its simplest forms, that love story plays out in one of three ways: Daughters either get their fathers' love, they don't get it, or they have that love and trust violated.

Daughters who get healthy, affectionate, and attentive relationships with their fathers draw the long straw in life. These women cried tears of gratitude during our hours together. Their hearts are filled naturally. They feel an inner sense of sufficiency and calm.

Daughters who grow up with fathers who abuse or abandon them draw the short straw. When they cried with me, theirs were tears of anger and pain. Their hearts were broken by their fathers. And as they move through life, they often try to relieve those broken hearts with one kind of anesthesia or another, as their stories in this book reveal.

I also met daughters who had fathers who were somewhere in between these heroic and horrific dads. Some of these dads were present physically but were emotionally disengaged. Some were withdrawn or depressed. Others were simply ambivalent about their daughters and neglected them. These women cried tears of regret when we met, for the love that was close, yet just outside of their reach. These daughters got what I call "the long and the short of it" in their fathers.

Another pattern within these long-and-short relationships is the attentive father who simultaneously corrodes the relationship with his daughter through harsh parenting that leaves her scarred and resentful. These are the "Dr. Jekyll and Mr. Hyde" fathers who build relationships and destroy them at the same time.

I heard from these women who got "the long and the short of it" that they feel a more insidious pain; its cause is muddled. It's harder to identify, recognize, and feel neglect than the shock and horror of abuse.

These women and their stories changed me forever. The short straw stories filled me with a sense of urgency in helping to inform fathers and daughters as widely as I could. The long straw stories helped show a path forward with their rich examples of spectacular fathering. So this work became a crusade to share as widely as possible what I'd learned, and to do it through the storytelling that had fired a dart into my heart and shaped me into a different father.

The Long Straw

She might not understand why you are happy or angry, dishonest or affectionate, but you will be the most important man in her life forever. When she is 25, she will mentally size her boyfriend or husband up against you. When she is 35, the number of children she has will be affected by her life with you. The clothes she wears will reflect something about you. Even when she is 75, how she faces her future will depend on some distant memory of time you spent together. Be it good or painful, the hours and years you spend with her—or don't spend with her—change who she is.

Meg Meeker, MD
Strong Fathers, Strong Daughters

Early in my work on this book, I called a friend to see if she would share her story. Before hanging up she asked me, "Do your daughters appreciate that they drew the long straw when it comes to fathers?" I was touched and flattered. But I knew that she knew only part of my story.

I was running marketing for a $600-million-a-year high technology company. I was a depressed, irritable, middle-aged man, who lived for Fridays and who woke up every Sunday morning in a state of dread because I had only 24 hours left to live; on Monday morning I would have to return to the spiritual death bed that was my job. By Sunday night, I usually had a knot in my stomach.

One day my wife Meg went to see an intuitive advisor named Bev.

1

During their time together, Bev got a vision of me at work. And then she began to cry. Twenty years after earning an MBA, I had what appeared to be a successful career, I projected a composed, confident persona, and had what most people probably saw as a wonderful family life. Privately I lived a life of misery. I hated my job. My life felt hard. My marriage was suffering. The dad shaping my two daughters was a depressed, irritable, and anxious man. That was the environment their young minds were marinating in, and I knew there were consequences to that. Another wakeup call, shortly after my wife's visit with Bev, further changed my life trajectory.

One morning I was slowly coming through that hazy state between sleep and wakefulness when my mind asked, "Do I have to get up? What day is it?" As I emerged from my dream state, another voice in my head replied, "Today is Monday. So you need to get up for work." Two words involuntarily came up from my gut and out my mouth.

"Oh, fuck," I said. My mind had awakened enough to have the realization that, "Today I have to go back to work," that pretend life that I hate yet dutifully march through, like a zombie in emotional quicksand. "Oh, fuck!"

I was trapped, of course, in a life of my own creation. My implicit career strategy was to work hard, even if it meant living in a state of perpetual dread, so I could earn enough money to someday escape dread. I was living an emotionally impoverished life so I could save enough money to escape an emotionally impoverished life. It's a common story among fathers everywhere.

There are many of us, these dead men walking. We spew a toxic emotional fog into our homes and families. We slowly poison them and ourselves, following an inner compass whose magnetic fields got scrambled as we came into adulthood.

I had this Monday wakeup call in February. In May, I hit the end of my corporate rope. I was burned out, ineffective, and disengaged. As part of a reorganization my position was eliminated. The same thing happened to one of my ex-bosses right after that. Today, literally as I write this, it happened to another executive there.

Any father raising his daughters within such a dark night of his soul is not giving them the long straw. I didn't even know what the long straw looked like. That's what set me upon this journey in the first place. I love my daughters so much; I want them to have a great dad. Deep inside, I feared they weren't getting one.

The following stories and others that I heard over my year's interviews showed me first-hand what those long-straw fathers are made of and what they do. These stories took my understanding of what it means to be a girl, a daughter, and a woman and inflated it like a balloon. These women and the intimate histories they shared changed my life. I hope they do the same for other fathers, in every corner of the world where a man says to himself, "I want to give my daughter more." And I want the stories to give validation to women, in the hope that they and their fathers can come together and find a greater wholeness that is available to each when they can give voice to their own experience and take seriously the experience of each other.

Daughter of the Great Depression

When I told Lucille about the work I was doing, she wanted to talk about her dad. In her eighties, she still drives and is as sharp as a tack. During our interview she shared clear memories of growing up during the Great Depression, and how that adversity shaped her parents and family.

Born in 1889 in Lansing, Michigan, Lucille's father Herman fought in the First World War and later worked for the Toledo Scale Co. in Toledo, Ohio. Lucille told me that some of her earliest memories were of her father's affection. "I can remember, as a baby, standing on his shoes and we would dance. And I remember the physical feeling of lying on his chest and his humming or singing to me. I remember the vibrations, and I still can feel that. It's like it was just a moment ago.

"The way my dad treated Mother was wonderful. He would always say, 'You're so beautiful' or 'You just look so pretty today' even when they were old. He'd bring her little surprises, tiny little things, put them in her hand. He really loved her."

Lucille's relationship with her father was one of such warmth, and the love she still feels for him is such a part of her, that she transformed physically as we spoke. Her face lit up; her skin tone changed. As her smile widened, her complexion became a rich color

5

of pink, and the wrinkles in her skin disappeared, as if her mind and body were being flushed with bliss.

Lucille's father raised bees in a lot beside the family's home. A musician, teacher, and conductor later in her life, she reminisced about how he used the bees to teach her an important lesson. "My mother was very afraid, but I loved it. He took me out to the bees and he'd let the bees land on him. He never was stung. He said you have to be calm inside because they can tell if you're afraid or nervous. And I remember my dad saying, 'You like them and they'll like you.' And that stood me well when I had to conduct before or with some famous people."

Among her early memories is her father putting her, as a toddler, inside the bell of his tuba. "I can remember the feeling of that metal. And he's blowing in there and making my skirt go up. It tells something about my dad and me. I thought this was just great."

Her father's playful spirit was demonstrated when Lucille was four. "We lived on a cement street, but it had cracks in the cement and they would put tar in those. I had learned to do a headstand, and I went out on that tar, which was soft in the warm summer sun, and did a headstand. I remember hearing my mother scream. She came out and I'm upside down with my head in the tar. She got some kind of stuff and made me sit in the bathtub with my hair in a pail for a long time. And my dad laughed and told me I shouldn't have done that."

As a small girl, Lucille watched as the houses in her neighborhood added a new cast of daytime characters—husbands and fathers—as the Great Depression ravaged Toledo. One day she asked her father, "Why are all the other daddies sitting on their porches?"

"Because they don't have any other place to go," he replied.

Her father kept his job, but at half salary, and the family lost their home. Herman refused to surrender his spirit. "My father said, 'We're going to have a new place to live. It's going to be really interesting.' Well, my mother's family had an old farmhouse that tenants lived in. It was filthy and the people who had been in there misused the bathtub for a toilet. And my mother broke. She was never the same. She cried and began to drink a lot. And my father was just as solid as a rock.

"Now here's the part that's going to blow your bloomers off and may sadden you: We're in this awful farmhouse. And at Christmas we had stockings of candy. And there were mice that came in the house and ate the candy. My mother cried and cried. And my dad decided to fix it. There was no money, just his little salary. And he found a vacant lot, and bought it for next to nothing, because nobody had any money.

"Then he found an old abandoned schoolroom sort of house a couple of blocks from his lot and he got that for almost nothing. And he dug a whole, full basement by hand, and put in cement block walls and a cement floor measured exactly to hold the house. And they moved that house to our lot on trucks and logs. I didn't know how it worked but everybody in the whole place was out watching and just amazed at it. They slowly moved it and rolled it somehow down the street. Dad's foundation was just miraculous; he had measured it so carefully that they just set it right down on the basement.

"And we saw that. My dad did that with his hands, in the night, and on Sundays, and he made a lovely home. He painted it and he wallpapered it, and he built stuff for us."

Lucille's story also was among those I heard that taught me how small things make the big difference for daughters. Behind their new family home, her father built a garage and workshop. "He would always go out after supper and work," Lucille recalled. "I would go out there, little snake that I was, and say, 'What's that tool for?' And he'd say, 'Why don't you learn how to use that?' And he made me process what these things were for.

"I was always welcomed to his workshop and that was a wonderful place I could go, and ask anything I wanted. And he would show me things, and he taught me how to refinish furniture, how to prepare it and what care it takes. I learned a lot of patience from him. When I was ten, I did my first piece, which is a desk I have in the bedroom now."

Lucille shared more stories of small things making a big difference in her life. "We lived right on Lake Erie, and there were piers that went out into the lake. And during the northeasters in the winter, it would be frozen and the rain and the ice would come flying in. My dad would wrap me all up, and he'd carry me out, we'd go walk out on the pier. And he'd hold me really tight. And the wind would just rock us. Oh, he'd laugh! It was so good and it was so scary and it was so fun. We shared adventures like that.

"He always had time to talk to me. I'd ask him about everything. I'd wonder about things, about how they worked, and I just remember him as being willing to talk about things. I knew that whatever I asked him was not dumb, that it was okay not to know something and to ask a question."

Lucille learned toughness from her father beginning at an early age. It helped her persevere through the challenges she encountered in the years ahead.

"I was fairly good doing physical things, and he wanted me to do sports because he was really talented. My mother would say, 'I don't like you to scrape up your knees because we're going to be singing at the program next Thursday night.' And Dad would say, 'Get in there and fight him! If you're doing tag or something, get in there!' And I broke my collarbone after flying into a tree one time and he said, 'Well, that's what happens.'

"When I was very little and starting to sing on the stage, he took me and a wash pail down to a theater. And my dad took me up on the stage and said, 'Okay, now I want you to sing this song. There's no piano, just sing it for me. And I'm going to go in the back of the auditorium and listen. Nothing is going to interrupt you, no matter what happens.' And so I started singing and my dad came down the aisle with this wash pan beating it and it was a horrible sound. I kept singing.

"And my dad said, 'That was good!' He was trying to teach me that when you're in front of an audience, people do awful things. They throw up, fall on the floor, have fits, scream, say dirty words, make fun of your music, throw stuff at you. And you are above that. That was useful in the church, when I was a minister later on.

"We had a saxophone in the house and I'd been fooling around with it, so my dad said, 'Well, you've got to have lessons.' So he arranged for me to take lessons. I started a band a couple years later. That was in the '40s, so a lot of the band guys were in the services. I had a high school all-guy band. I also took jobs by myself, like if someone needed an alto sax player.

"When I was fifteen or sixteen, I got a call to play in a club. As usual, Dad took me and stayed near the band stand. The band and waiters had to use the back door at the end of the night. In the alley was this guy who was just in a knife fight. He had his ear cut off and was bleeding all over. My dad said, 'Just put your head up and keep walking.' It was another lesson.

"What I learned from my dad was nobody was going to do this for me. When I graduated, my high school band director said I should audition for this event, and I said okay. I had to make some money. It was 3,000 girls from across the US who tried out for this band to play with the Cleveland Browns. I auditioned and I made it. I was eighteen years old. We had our own train car that went wherever the team went, and we sang and danced and made a lot of money, a lot for me, anyway. I saved enough to go to school for one semester. I didn't have a quarter from anywhere, except what I could make.

"I remember, coming back to go to college, I had my saxophone, but I couldn't afford the food. So I got the guy who was in charge of the dining hall to just let me have breakfast and supper. The next year I just had supper. And I found a restaurant that would give me two slices of bread for five cents and I could have ketchup on it and water. That's how I did it. I fainted sometimes. I just didn't have enough food. I couldn't afford it. I weighed 81 pounds. And I remember thinking, 'I can do this.' At Christmas, the only way I could go home would be to hitchhike. That's how I got home whenever I did. I hitchhiked alone, at 81 pounds.

"My school had an outstanding jazz band, so I tried out for that and they invited me to play, which was an honor. They'd never had a woman before. And I thought that was one of the things I could do to eat; you could make fifteen, twenty dollars. That was big time.

"Then the dean of women called me into her office and said, 'Do I understand correctly that you were considering playing in the jazz band?' I said, 'Yes, that's what I do as my work and that's how I got to college.' And she said, 'Well, no nice girl would do that sort of thing. I know what they do in those band buses when they go to play.'

"Okay, now here's where something from my Dad clicked in. I remember saying to this dowager lady, 'My dad said you can choose to be good or be bad, whether you're in a band or even if you're a Dean of Women.'

"She said, 'If you play in that band again, you not only will be kicked out of here, you will not get in any state school in Ohio.' Which would mean that I could not go to school.

"That hurt, and it was wrong. It was just coming up toward St. Patrick's Day, and my Irish was up. The Dean of Women always walked into the dining room first and filled her glass with milk and got her food and sat down. Well, I just happened by the drugstore, and picked something up. And before the suppertime I took this little vial and poured it into the milk canister. And so when the dean of women went and poured her glass and it came out bright green, she screamed. It was so great."

Lucille had to give up the jazz band to stay in school. She got a typing job at 35 cents an hour in a university office. "I thought about my dad, digging the basement, and persisting. So all of that is kind of like something that he gave me."

Lucille's father died in 1956, while still living in the home he'd created. At the time, Lucille had a young baby and was also taking care of her sick mother. She was so immersed in those responsibilities that she didn't mourn her father's loss. Then she saw the tubas at a parade a year after his death.

"My dad took me to every parade that he could find. And he would put me up on his shoulders and I was taller than anyone. And he'd say, 'I think those are the tubas!'

"I went to this parade by myself and I broke down and just cried and cried and cried and cried. It was a wonderful piece of time right there."

As Lucille spoke of her father, I found myself wishing I had known him. He had an uncommon breadth of strength and sensitivity. He was a man who worked seven days a week, who built a home with his ingenuity and bare hands, yet who had the tenderness to tell his wife she was beautiful, and to bring her small gifts, even as she withdrew into alcohol and depression.

I fell in love with what Lucille's father gave her. While her mother was telling Lucille to not scrape her knees, her father told her not to worry about scraping her knuckles out in the world.

Lucille and I have stayed in touch since our interview. At a recent gathering, she told me about a dream she'd had that she said was related to our conversations. In the dream, she is standing and facing a large wall, the type that would circle an old European city. To her left the wall stretches as far as she can see. It is "graceful, colorful, and lovely," she says. To the right, the wall is taller, plain, and heavier, like a buttress. And it ends well within sight. We talk about that wall as the timeline of her life, with her long colorful past, and her shorter future ahead to her right.

Lucille then sees a door handle immediately in front of her. My hand appears, then I do, and turning the handle down, I pull the door open toward us. Lucille looks through the opening in the wall. She doesn't see anything specific, but recalls the peaceful, comforting feelings as she prepares to step through. "Oh, good," she says to herself. "This is going to be okay."

Out of Africa

I know I'Satta from an inner-city church we both attend. I thought she would be perfect for an interview as I began searching for women of African ancestry. When I asked her if she would be interested, she said she had quite a story to tell, and invited me to her home to share it.

I'Satta emigrated to the US from Liberia in her twenties, and was 50 years old when we spoke. She is married and is the mother of three girls and two boys. She had recently left her job as a human resource manager to begin a day care business.

Her father Gardiah was born in Liberia in 1925, the third of four brothers, in a small town on Africa's west coast. After attending vocational school he began working as an auto mechanic. Soon after, at the age of twenty, he married a woman who was eighteen.

I'Satta said her parents were poor, with nothing except their hard work and love for each other. Their first two children died shortly after birth. Born in 1959, I'Satta was the sixth of eight surviving children.

Working for the government, Gardiah progressed through the ranks to become a chief procurement officer. He and his wife bought land, then built houses and apartment complexes which they rented for income. When I'Satta was seven, the family had enough money to send her to a private boarding school. Given how challenging her family's economic circumstances were, her father made sure his children made the most of their opportunities.

"At the end of every term, you would go home. If you did very well, he would tell you congratulations. But he thought Bs were not good. Especially B-minuses. He wanted us to do better. And he set up a reward system. If you made an A, he'd maybe give you five dollars. A-plus he would give you seven dollars, B-plus he would give you maybe four or three. Anything after that he'd say you failed, you didn't do good. And his reasoning was you have nothing to do but to study. You don't have to work. All you have to do is concentrate on your lessons. And that made us want to do better, want to do better, want to do better. He had his way of bringing all of us around. He was good.

"My father was the disciplinarian of the family. He worked, so he wasn't home most of the time. My mother was home. And so if you did something and she told you, 'I will tell your father,' we did not want that! And when he got home, he had three strikes and you were out. And then you got severe punishment.

"Punishment could be a whupping. He loved to send people in their room under the bed. And no child likes to go under the bed because that isolates you. And if he put you under the bed, he'd put you under the bed in the morning when he was going to work, and you stayed under the bed all day. Some people went under the bed for a week. A week!

"You knew if he said, 'Go under the bed,' he meant for you to go under the bed. If you didn't, your punishment would triple. So eventually we learned it won't do any good to come from under that bed, because I'll just have to pay a bigger penalty.

"As I got older the relationship became stronger. Especially when I started to have children. Because I remember when I had my first child, I was eighteen. I was very young, just like my mother; it's a circle. I had my child out of wedlock. So he should have been mad and disappointed, but he wasn't. He took my oldest child like that was his favorite grandchild for a long time."

I'Satta absorbed her father's emphasis on discipline, and it shaped how she came to define herself as a woman. She also learned a tremendous sense of self-control. "I strongly believe being a disciplinarian or being the one in authority within the family does not have to refer necessarily to the sex. It has to refer to the personality of that parent. And the reason I say that is because in my family I think I am the disciplinarian.

"I tell you one good thing about my father. You know when there are many siblings growing up, there's always sibling rivalry, sibling confrontation? When my father came home, there were always complaints. Maybe one sister had done this to another sister, but there was one thing he always taught us: You have to have a huge sense of control. No matter how angry you are, if your sister hit you during the day, you're not supposed to hit her back. You constrain yourself. You move away from her and you wait until he came.

"And when my father came and you went to him, you couldn't go to him with anger, either. He wouldn't listen to you. He'd say, 'You have to go drink a glass of water and when your temper cools down, come and tell me what made you mad. I will not be able to understand you while you're mad.' So one of the greatest things I learned from my father was that huge sense of control. And I learned that it could be learned, it was a habit that could be developed.

"I have a high sense of control. I can be angry and sit here and you'd never know I'm angry. I will vent at the appropriate time in the appropriate manner to the appropriate person. If you don't have that sense of control, your anger will allow you to be nobody. Because anger is something that takes control over you and allows you to lose yourself.

"When you brought your complaint, most times children tell what the other party did and he would say, 'What did you do?' And then he'd set you aside, he'd tell you to go to a separate room and he'd call your sibling and say, 'What happened?' And that sibling would explain. And then he would ask, 'What did you do?' And usually there would be something extracted from both persons. And he'd bring two of you together in the same room. 'Okay, she told me this that you did not tell me. Did this happen?'

"'Yes it did.'

"'Why did you extract it? A story told that is incomplete is not a story. You need to say everything that happened so that I can be abreast of the situation.' Then he went to the next person. Then he would ask each of you, 'In the final analysis, what could you have done better, or what could you have done differently?' So if my father told you that you were getting punished, whatever punishment he gave you was a punishment he stood by. I learned that. It helped structure my life.

"Through his examples my father taught me to love my children unconditionally. He came to see us at school every Sunday. If we were sick, our mother made the meals, she gave us the baths, she laid us down, but our father would be right there. When I grew up, I didn't see many fathers attach themselves to their children.

"There is a belief outside of third world countries that some parents invest more time and resources into their boys than into their daughters. That wasn't the case with us. Our father treasured his daughters, I want to say even more than he treasured his boys. A neighbor used to say you couldn't mess with my father's daughters.

"So he taught me the value of family life, he taught me the importance of loving and going above and beyond to provide for your family. When you grow up in an environment where resources are not readily available, and you have to struggle very hard to get it, I think when you do achieve it, you see it from a different perspective. So that's why the way he loved us meant so much to us."

I'Satta's father taught her much about her economic lot in life. First, that it didn't define who she is, and second, that anyone could move beyond their material position through hard work. "Our parents told us that nobody is better than another person. They had this philosophy where they would tell us that regularly. Circumstances and situations could be better, but nobody's better than another person. So because somebody across the street is more wealthy than you are does not make you inferior.

"One step beyond that, you can get to be where they are if you work hard. Our parents instilled the passion for hard work. The ability to want to achieve, to want to excel, to want to make life better, to not be content, to always remind us of where they came from.

"They told us stories about how when they were newly married they took palm tree branches and built a little house, a hut, when they bought their land. And when the rains came, they would move from one eave of the house to the other, and the rain would be pouring and my father would be outside and she's inside showing him where the rain's coming from. Plus they had babies in the house.

"So they always told us these stories to show us where they started from and where they got to. And you only get there by hard work and perseverance."

I'Satta's father died in 1980 of a brain tumor. She was 24. "It was difficult watching him in pain. We would tell him, 'Why don't you just get out of bed and come outside and sit down?' and he'd say, 'I'm just in so much pain, I can't.' We watched him slowly die.

"It has been 29 years since my father died and I'm not exaggerating, it's like it was just yesterday. So every year April 9th, I wake up in the morning, I wake everybody up in this house, I'm crying. I still miss my father." I'Satta has been crying for a few minutes, and now begins sobbing. "I still miss my father. I wish he was here with me. I have more children for him to love. I hope he's in a better place.

"I remember I dreamed about him and he had told me to come and go with him some place. And I was going and he disappeared. He just disappeared in the dream, even though he and I were talking. I knew he was dead.

"Every April 9th when I start to cry in this house, my kids say, 'What's wrong, Mama?' And when I say it's April 9th, they go, 'Mama, you can't be doing that! It's been too long! Come on now, Mama.'

And I say, 'You just don't know. Go in that room and hug your daddy. Kiss him. 'Cause for me, it will never be.'"

I was struck by the brand of tough love that I'Satta's father gave his children. He was strong. He instilled discipline. He came home from work and marshaled the energy to work as the supreme court justice of the household, forcing each squabbling child to present a complete story along with his or her grievance. At the same time, he had a heart full of love.

I saw I'Satta's father within her. Anyone who looks closely can see him. She is a beautiful, sensitive, feminine woman. And yet she has a steely gaze and powerful presence that she can turn on instantly. I want my daughters to have that. That became clear to me as I took in I'Satta's story. If I wanted my daughters to have an on-switch for power, I needed to model it, I realized.

I'Satta was one of the first women, but certainly not the only one, to share in so many words that her father helped fill her with masculine energy. And as their stories unfolded, I came to see that imparting masculinity to my daughters had been one of my blinds spots.

Farm Worker's Daughter

I found most of the women I interviewed for this book. Blanca Estela Zarazúa found me. She read about my project when it was mentioned in Berkeley's alumni magazine. She contacted me shortly after that, and offered to fly to Portland for an interview.

Born in 1956, Blanca is the daughter of a Mexican agricultural worker; she put herself through law school at Santa Clara University, then the MBA program at Berkeley. She is an attorney and a US Honorary Consul for Mexico, based in Salinas, California.

Blanca invited me to meet her at an airport hotel. When I arrived, we sat down in the living room of her suite, and began to talk. I always eased into my interviews, particularly with women I'd never met. We talked about therapy; that this wasn't therapy, but that I wanted to know how much, if any, they had done around their relationships with their fathers. Knowing that in advance had an enormous impact on how I handled the most sensitive issues that came up.

About ten minutes after I met Blanca, I noticed that her eyes were tearing. She was beginning to cry. And we had not even begun our interview. Such was the bond of affection she felt with her father. Her pain was particularly acute because he had died within the year before she and I met. Grief is the price we pay for love lost. And Blanca, without question, loved her father. He was a quiet hero, a simple man, and a stunning father. She grieved deeply for more than four hours that we spent together.

Born in Santa Catarina, Guanajuato, in the central part of Mexico, Blanca's father Aquilino Zarazúa came to the Salinas Valley in 1945 as a guest agricultural worker under the US / Mexico bracero program. Blanca lived in both countries as a girl while her father worked on farms and ranches.

Later, someone recommended him for a job working at a wealthy family's private ranch in the Carmel Valley. "My mother was the maid at the main house and my dad was the gardener," Blanca recalled. "We were raised in the servants' quarters. It was a very healthy, wholesome upbringing in every way, very bi-cultural. People around us were very supportive of our hopes of excelling in education. My father said that he came to this country to educate his daughters; he stayed in this country to educate his daughters and that was the main objective of being here. All three of us graduated from college.

"It was a very traditional Mexican upbringing, very Catholic. On weekends we would go to East Salinas, which is heavy agricultural, low income. During the week, I took piano lessons. We didn't have furniture or anything; I'd go up to the main house and practice on the piano there. So, I could be practicing a violin-piano duet in Pebble Beach one day and the next day, I'd be on the east side of Salinas with very low income people who lived in trailers or whatever, packed into labor camps. So it was a very diverse socioeconomic perspective that we were given."

Blanca and I went back to her earliest memories of times she shared with her father.

"When it would thunder and I would get scared, he said, 'God's a little upset, but He's going to be fine. It's going to stop soon.' And people tell me now that I would never go to sleep until he got home, that I had to be in his arms. I just couldn't sleep without him first putting me into bed. So, I'd sit in his lap and then he would carry me.

He was always giving positive feedback when I was a kid. I would go to home ec class and bring ghastly sandwiches with black olives and stuff. And he'd always say the right thing, that they're great, and you know he was puking.

"When we were teenagers, my dad took us to Mexico to see where he had been born. We went on mule. That was the only way to get to this hut up on this mountain where he was raised. And then, a few days later, he took us to a four-star hotel in Acapulco, to show us that Mexico's got a little bit of everything and it's very diverse. It was very wise on his part.

"The people who owned the private ranch left for Santa Barbara, and we had to leave that home where my parents, my two sisters, and I lived in the servants' quarters. We moved away and my father started one of the first, if not *the* first, gardening businesses on the Monterey Peninsula. My father did some work for the new owners of the ranch and they told my father they were planning on demolishing the servants' quarters. He begged with them to not demolish the home, as he had raised his daughters there. And they sold the home to my dad."

Much like I'Satta's family, Blanca's put a premium on education, and she took that to heart. "As an immigrant child, it's often communicated, not in words, that if you're the smartest kid in the family, you have to kind of bring back social redemption and be an engineer or a doctor or a lawyer or something 'real.' I felt subconsciously that I had to do something professional. In Mexico, titles are very important. You say Engineer Zarazúa or Attorney Zarazúa or some designation. I really felt that pressure to do something real for the family, because we had had such little formal education in our family.

"When I went to college, I would get checks from people in the community, because they had been following my progress. My parents were well known for being so hard-working and kind that everybody was just rooting for us.

"I went to Santa Clara's law school and did very well in law review and moot court. I always looked at education as a privilege. My MBA was at Berkeley and my thesis was in tax. During my last semester of law school, I worked at the California Supreme Court as an intern and then I clerked there. I worked at Bank of America as a tax lawyer for four years, which gave me skills that I'm using now, in terms of not being intimidated by that environment and all the nuances and what you're supposed to do and not do in that context."

When she was in her thirties, Blanca's father had a major heart attack. She did "the very Mexican thing for a daughter," she said. She moved back to the ranch house to care for her parents. While taking care of her father, she started a practice with a law firm in Monterey. Soon, she met the Consul General in San Jose and shortly after that she was appointed honorary consul to Mexico.

Like I'Satta's father, Blanca's was a man with an unusual ability to move from hard to soft, between strength and sensitivity. With little more to sell than his capacity for hard physical labor, he was driven to succeed financially, tenacious in his dedication to get his daughters educated.

"One of my dad's younger sisters got pregnant, and Dad was re-ally supportive of her. My mother and I wonder where he gets this whole sense of being more supportive than twenty-first century men would be to women, just crazy, crazy. He's always said that if you educate a mom, you educate a family; you have to educate the girls. He was a very wise person. He had a tremendous, uncanny sense of tact and sensitivity in terms of communication. He always knew what to say, when to say it, how much to say. And it was just artful.

"He would run into people that he had worked with at a young age and they would just start crying, crying about the emotional recall over the arduous work that they had to undertake. It's illegal now. You just aren't allowed to work that hard anymore, because it's cruel. It's mind boggling to think how much he persevered in a physical way. He had a tremendous drive and persistence and willingness to work a thousand hours a day, if necessary, to get where he needed to get.

"And they had nothing else but their arms. These were their assets. That was their resume. When they would be interviewed, they would look at their palms and if they weren't crispy and chunky, it's like 'Get out of here. You haven't been working and you're not going to work.'

"I remember that when people say, 'Oh, you're working all weekend.' Yeah, I got a soda and a heater and lighting and a computer. I'm just using my brain that I'd be using anyway. I'm not out in the field.

"My seeing firsthand his struggle helped me. It's not just about telling your kid that it's rough. It's living it. And it's non-negotiable that you have to keep going. No matter how bored or tired or upset you are, you have to keep going. And that's what's given me my resilience.

"I have met so many ridiculously cruel fathers in my work that it makes me appreciate even more how fortunate I have been. Child abusers, domestic violence, I've seen it all. And it just makes me say, 'God, did I get lucky. I am so lucky.'"

Two weeks before Blanca's father died, he wanted to go to Tijuana. She said she would take him, to which her mother replied, "You're crazy."

"I said, 'I'm crazy, but I'm taking him to Tijuana.' So, I got two ladies to go with me and we took him to Tijuana. He was weak the whole time, except when we went to a Brazilian restaurant that I really liked. And he had a couple of shots of tequila. He acted like he was 50 years old again. And that made the whole trip worthwhile."

During the last week of her father's life, Blanca stayed home with him. "I didn't bathe. I didn't sleep. I sat in the bed with him in the living room. And we were communicating all the time. I kept thinking, and it's more beautiful in Spanish, but I wanted to bottle his breathing. His breathing gave me some assurance, like he's still alive. So, I called my office and I taped his breathing as a voice message. I still have it there. And when I need a little boost, I just listen to his breathing.

"That last week, I rode back home in the ambulance with him.

And I was telling him all the ranches that we were driving by that he had worked, just so he could feel that he was passing on top of that land that he had worked."

Blanca had no trouble identifying what she absorbed from her father. "He gave me the ability to give strength to others. And it's not through words. It's a pretty fabulous story of perseverance and capitalizing on what you have inside as a person and what your external environment is offering you. I took so many values, of being a person of your word, being punctual, being honest, being respectful, doing the impossible to get the job done, whatever the assignment is, just get it done, persevere, persevere, in the light of adversity. Don't give up and be very proud of your roots, of your heritage, do not be ashamed. And I never have been.

"And without his sacrifice and without my ability to see firsthand his sacrifice, I wouldn't be as persistent and driven and feisty and tolerant and compassionate as I am. My positive qualities come from the struggle. And always because of that struggle, knowing that I am so privileged, I am so thankful. That's always my point of reference. I never lose sight of that.

"Even today, nobody says the M word anymore. Everybody says Latino. Well, I'm not a Latino consul. I'm a Mexican consul. Mexico is not a bad country and being Mexican is not a bad thing. You have to be proud of who you are, with all your defects and everything else. And you need to, in a quiet but very irrefutable, unequivocal way, show people what you're made of, who you are.

"He used to tell me that he would go to the big city with his dad and see all these important, educated people. He probably aspired to being that way, had he had the opportunity. So the next best thing would be to have his children be a part of that mix and be significant in society and certainly never struggle like he had to. Education is freedom, freedom to have choices and not have to work at McDonalds or pick strawberries."

Blanca was with her father when he died in the servants' quarters that became their family home. The first call she made after his death was to the former owners, thanking them for allowing him to keep the house and to raise his daughters there and to die there. Blanca and her family held the funeral in the garden.

I learned an important lesson from her—many, really, as I heard the story of her strong but humble father. It wasn't just his examples of hard work, sacrifice, or emphasis on educating his daughters. What really stuck with me was the answer I heard to my final question. I asked Blanca if there was anything she wanted from her father that she didn't get. She didn't hesitate at all before responding.

"More time."

Woman Raised
as a Son

Before we met, I had no idea what I would learn from Kim about parenting my daughters. Kim is transgender. She was born male, anatomically, and raised as a boy. Yet Kim defined herself as female for as far back as she can remember. Kim was, she recalled with me, a little girl struggling to live inside a boy's body.

Kim was 48 when we met for our interview, and had been through transgender surgery a decade earlier. There had to be a father-daughter story inside this woman raised as a boy, I thought to myself as I considered meeting her for the first time. And as different as her life had been from mine, I assumed she must have something to teach me: She was, after all, the only person I interviewed who has been both a father and a daughter.

Kim's identity has always been as a female, and I refer to her throughout this story as "she," regardless of whether the reference is to before or after her gender shift.

Kim was born in New York City, then studied physics and economics in college prior to a successful career as a business journalist, consultant, and business executive. Kim married and became a father of two children before the marriage ended in 2001. At 38 Kim went through a full gender change surgery and hormonal treatment, and like many who go through that process, lost her wife, children, job, and much more. At the same time, she gained a new and surprising relationship with her father.

Kim's father was born in Brooklyn in 1933 to immigrant parents from Ireland. After military service in the 1950s, he went to college on the GI Bill and studied accounting and finance. He worked his way up from a bank teller to the CEO of a Wall Street firm. During our time together, I found Kim to be full of important lessons from both her biological father and a surrogate father she met in her early teens.

In her childhood relationship with her biological father, Kim told me about growing up with a sense of loss, of not being known. "I felt like I would never be known and I would never be understood, that he would never know that he had a daughter and not a son. You just shut it down. You decide as a five-year-old, 'It must be my lot in life not to express this essential aspect of me. My essential nature is not to be expressed.'

"I felt like it was my job to be a boy, even if it was just a day job. My dad and I used to watch Star Trek, the original one. And Mr. Spock was a half-human, half-Vulcan. So the boy part of me was the Vulcan and the girl was the human. And just like Mr. Spock, I was always suppressing the human, so that was sort of my metaphor. That helped me a lot."

Kim's father was a traditional, conventional man in many respects, and someone she considered the person least likely to understand who she really was. He was a businessman, a former athlete and minor league baseball pitcher.

"My father was kind of offset from us, because of his career, because he was under so much pressure and because of his shy nature. So, we never knew him. And my reaction to all that was, 'I really can't be a boy, because I don't like men. I don't want to be one. It doesn't make sense for me.' I didn't want to incorporate masculine culture into myself, because it felt wrong. It felt like a loss, like a spiritual death."

While he wasn't a physically affectionate man, Kim's father was deeply grounded in principles, and she took from him numerous lessons that "came from the trunk of this tree of principle that he lived by. Integrity. Your word was your bond. Responsibility to those around you. Caution, not to be hasty or irrational.

"I didn't really wake up to those principles until I was in high school. I remember at about twelve or thirteen years old, all of a sudden feeling that my dad had given me a model that I could use to process and manage my own experience. As a teenager, you start to confront more complex situations, morally ambiguous situations or behaviors of your friends or people that you knew in school that were not good: drinking and driving, getting involved with girls or boys. There was all this additional complexity. And there were things like opportunities to cheat in school that every kid has."

Through a foreign exchange program, Kim came to meet a Chilean surrogate father who was blessed with qualities that complemented her father's. "My Chilean father was a really important man in my life. He was born on an island in the Patagonia in 1906, raised six sons, and owned seven or eight industries—metallurgy, truck manufacturing, bus manufacturing, railroads, logging, delivery and transportation, import/export."

Kim lived with this Chilean family for several months between eighth and ninth grade. "I started this relationship with this dear man—he was probably about 70—and he was vigorous and masculine and he treated me like his own son.

"He was also a man of principle, like my father. But he was much more of an extrovert about his masculinity, much more fierce. He used to call himself The Old Lion. He was raised and educated in German schools. He insisted on the highest standards of discipline and practice in his own children, and he taught me a lot of really important lessons about setting intentions and going for those intentions and being determined and persevering in achieving those things."

As a teenager, Kim worked on Wall Street during the summers. She would commute with her father each day, and absorb his principles through the stories he would tell. "It was just the two of us, so I had hours and hours of time with my dad, leaving the house at seven, getting home at seven o'clock at night. And he would tell me stories of his travails and his challenges running these companies. Wall Street's full of liars and scoundrels. It's full of wheeler-dealers and haymakers, men of principle, every different type.

"He would talk about various people and tell me how he thought about that person. But he always did it from the point of view of how they're behaving and what their needs are and how their behavior and their needs are taking them in a direction where they're not going to get their needs met, or how this was a person of principle and they were going to get their reward, because they acted from principle. He was staging these morality plays in the car and showing me the denouement of what would happen when all was said and done. It was like a continuous stream of Wall Street parables.

"So my biological father was someone who was always building things, like his life was an office building and he was building it one floor at a time. It was all very measured and cautious. My Chilean father is sort of a Jim Kirk character, much more swashbuckling, a ladies' man. He recited Spanish poetry to my mother when he visited. So here are two completely different versions of a principled man: one, the taciturn, beautiful, shy man, who never really shows himself to anyone unless you're really looking and then this Lord Byron kind of guy. And so I had both of those people.

"From my father, I picked up the principles I described. And from my Chilean father, I picked up that everything you do is important. Every decision you make should never be taken lightly. If you're not ambitious, you're not really living. When I was in Chile, I would go for walks with him and we would talk in Spanish and he would impart these stories. And he was such a powerful, beautiful man, just a poet and a philosopher and a giant on the Chilean stage."

Adulthood brought new complexities to this woman-inside-the-man. "When I got married, no one else in my family was producing heirs. I was the first one to have two children. So I became the heir of the family. I was the A student. I was the successful writer, the entrepreneur. I was doing all of these things to compensate for the agony that I felt inside. I was hyper-exceeding everything to please my father and assuage my failure to be a man.

"So then I came out and told my parents in a phone conversation that this was going on and that my marriage was falling apart because of it and that I was going to go through this process. And it was like a bomb going off in our family. That's the whole Irish thing, right? You never talk about anything. Although, to their credit, the most amazing thing about this is what happened to my relationship with my father after I told them.

"My oldest sister rallied to the cause. I gave her a book, Jenny Boylan's "She's Not There," which is a great book on this topic. She read this book and the lights went on and she got it. She sat down with everyone and explained everything that was going on. She said, 'You know, this is not Kim's fault. This is just what happened. We have to rally for her. She needs us right now.'

"So my father calls me up on the phone and says, 'I've thought about this a lot and I think you should go through with this. And to show you that I've concluded that this isn't your fault and isn't anything that you've done wrong—I understand the decisions that you felt you had to make and the ones that you have to make now—I want to pay for all of your surgeries.'

"It was unbelievable. My mother had her own struggles with it. I said, 'I'm having surgery in Arizona and it would be great if one of you could be there or both of you.' My mother, because mothers are physically part of their children, couldn't be there for that. But my dad's like, 'I'm going to be there.' So my dad arrived the day after I woke up and stayed for three days."

Her father's openness to that gender transformation began a seismic shift in their relationship, for it was then that Kim began to feel his deep and genuine acceptance. "The amazing thing is we talked about principle, and then the states of being that are beyond principle, where there's love.

"And what I discovered for the first time in the process of my gender shift was that my father really loved me. There was a whole other relationship that I had never been able to be aware of, because of the gender dysphoria. And there was a regret that I hadn't told him earlier, that when I was nineteen and I realized it, I should have told him, 'This is what's going on.' But I never told anyone. So this process has unfolded and my father is a totally different man to me now than he was then.

"When I was 22, I went to a Jungian therapist who was encouraging me to dream. And one of the dreams I came back with was that I was in a daylight basement with windows. And it was really sunny outside, but the basement had no lights. The walls were covered with green clay, like green stucco.

"In the middle of the room, there was a pedestal, like an Ionic column. And on the pedestal was a bust of my father's head. The eyes were real and he never talked. He was looking at me. I told him, 'I can no longer be who you need me to be. I have to be myself and I need to leave now.' And I left the room, walked up the stairs out into the light and it's the end of the dream.

"And the therapist said to me the next time I saw him, 'I think you're playing on the wrong team.' And I was already playing on the female team in my mind. That was a male metaphor. I didn't understand what that meant. What he was telling me was I needed to transition, but I thought he was telling me that I needed to go back and be on the boys' team, because I was already in my mind on the girls' team. I lost twenty years because of that confusion."

This liberation from her past and her preconceived notions of her father profoundly changed Kim's life. "I talk to my father probably three times a week on the phone. We have an impeccably close relationship. And he's been there for me so much. It gave me faith in the world that I never had. A former employee of mine once said,

'Before you came out and transitioned, I always referred to you as the boss with the mask.' I had my father's mask on. And now, I don't wear a mask.

"I remember in that whole period when my relationship with my father was changing, my cheeks were hurting all the time. And I was like, 'Oh, I must have some disease.' It was because I was smiling. It had been so long since I really smiled that the muscles in my cheeks were aching.

"It was like being given life all over again. It makes me want to cry when I think about it, because for so long, I didn't know that this beautiful spirit created me and was in my life. Because I had chosen to walk in darkness, I saw everyone else in a false light. It made me see the entire experience of my dad totally differently.

"He really had a lot to teach. He was never moralistic, but he was always deeply moral. He was fiercely loyal and loved the people who were loyal back. I always felt if I came out I'd lose all that loyalty, I would lose my father's love.

"What I gained was being able to call my father up on the phone and tell him I loved him and have him tell me he loved me back. And when he's dressed up to go out to a restaurant, I gained the ability to tell him he looked nice. I gained the freedom to be myself, finally, and to experience a pipeline of emotional riches. I love talking to him. I don't feel like I have to hide anything.

"I'm closer to my father than I am to almost anyone else. I want his advice on things. Finally in my life, I have this person who can know me. And the only way he can know me is if I trust and I share."

I was right in my assumption that I would have something to learn from Kim. Hers was one of those stories that brought to light the importance of a father imparting principles to his daughters. Kim was also clear on just how important her father's unconditional love and acceptance were to her.

In my conversation with Kim, I really felt for the first time the enormous need that a daughter has for a father who is attuned to her, fully open to who she is, and who will embrace and love her unconditionally. This helped me enormously as I wrestled with the notion of "tough love" and how great fathers seem to combine the two.

Kim was also one of my early teachers about another important dimension of the father-daughter relationship: The importance of openness and authenticity, and how those create a tipping point in relationships. There were more such stories for me to hear in the months ahead.

Will You
Marry Me?

Wendy didn't feel very safe with the thought of meeting me. I couldn't blame her; she didn't know me from the man on the moon. A mutual acquaintance, whom neither of us knew well, suggested that she call me. When she did, she was guarded. I told her we should meet for coffee first, then she could see if she felt comfortable scheduling an interview.

I met at coffee shops with many of the women who didn't know me. I was starting with a zero balance in my trust account with them and asking if they would let me into a place in their lives that many of them had never shared before.

Over coffee, I gave Wendy the names of women who had offered themselves as references. I gave her the office address where we'd meet and told her to share it with a friend before our interview. I told her to bring her cell phone, to call a friend once we got in my office, to tell him or her exactly where she was, and to give them my cell phone number, too. It took a few weeks, but Wendy finally agreed to meet. As we did, she told me about the first man she ever fell in love with.

Wendy's father was born in Pittsburgh in the late 1930s. Of Russian Jewish heritage, he grew up in the Squirrel Hill area of Pittsburgh as an only child. A cousin twenty years older served as his surrogate brother and father. Wendy told me that her father was an extremely bright child—so bright, in fact, that he was considered odd by teachers and the other kids. Teachers told his parents not to expect much of him, that "My dad was somewhere close to mental retardation. They said, 'Get him into a trade school.' My grandparents were unwilling to accept that diagnosis and they took him to Carnegie Mellon to have his IQ tested. And the therapist came down after an hour with my dad and said, 'I'm not sure how high his IQ is going to be, but he's not an idiot.'

"My dad has an IQ in the 160s, I think. And he said that the IQ test results changed everything for him. Because prior to that, everyone sort of looked at him as this weird kid and after that he was the smart kid, and that was a much better identity to have and one that gave him respect. A lot of the validation he got in his life came from how smart he is."

Wendy's parents met as students at Oberlin College. "I think they were each other's first love. It was a challenging match because my dad had swarthy skin, black curly hair, heavy Russian Jewish features. And my mom's family was Midwest, Illinois, Southern Baptists."

Her parents relocated to Chicago while her father attended medical school, and married shortly after that. "I don't think my dad was crazy about my mom having me," Wendy said. "He was in med school; he was freaked out and overwhelmed; it was very intense."

More than any woman I met with, Wendy was able to recall vividly her early childhood infatuation with her father. "My earliest memories of him come from when I was about three and four. He wasn't around much because he was doing this internship, and he had those ridiculous hours. So he showed up and I was all over him. I just adored him.

"I remember when my dad was shaving, and sitting on the tank lid of the toilet, with my feet on the lid of the toilet seat. And I proposed: 'I want you to marry me when I grow up!' He said, 'Um, well, you know, here's the thing. When you grow up, you're not going to want to marry me.' And I started to cry. Because I could feel there was a 'No' in there. And I said, 'Yes, I will.'

"And he said, 'You really won't. First, I'm your dad, and second, you'll want to marry someone your own age.' And I was crying, 'But I wanna marry you!'"

Wendy began to cry. "I'm surprised that I'm crying. It's the Electra complex...attachment and affection at that age, the little girl wants to marry and be with her father forever. I wanted him to be my guy."

When she was four, Wendy and her family moved to San Francisco for her father's residency at UC San Francisco Medical Center. "He wasn't around a lot, and when he was, I was just so excited. And I have really sweet memories of that time, getting into bed with them in the mornings, opening my mom's eyelids with my finger and whispering in her face, 'Are you awake?' And I used to get up on the bed and stand over my dad quietly and then count to three and sit down on his stomach as hard as I could because I liked the way he would 'Ugh!' What a terrible way to wake up! I only got away with that twice."

Wendy grew up with a left-brain father and a right-brain mother, who was an artist and model. It was not an easy pairing. "My parents' marriage dissolved for a whole bunch of reasons. It was the '60s, they were both feeling sexually adventurous, my dad in particular, and I think that contributed to the dissolution of their marriage. But my mom left to go be with another man, and left me with my dad.

"So my dad was a medical resident and suddenly had this five-year-old girl full-time. And I'm sure it was like *Kramer vs. Kramer*, where in the beginning it's, 'How do you feed them, what do you do with them?' If I wasn't already in love with my dad, that was when I fell in love with him, when my mom was gone and it was just us.

"I remember the mornings. He would make coffee for himself, and then he would make me a cup that had a teeny bit of coffee and a lot of milk and sugar. And I would sit on his lap and he would have just showered, so he smelled like soap and wet hair. And he would read me the funnies and we would drink our coffee."

Wendy's parents came back together shortly after that, and tried to reconcile their marriage. It didn't last. Wendy recalled in detail one of her life's most painful moments. "I got up one morning, wearing my white flannel nightgown that was a little too short; it was washed out but it had little roses. I had long hair in a braid and the braid was coming loose. And I remember walking down the hallway, waking up, and it was like they'd stayed up all night packing. I walked out and my mom was on my left and my dad was on my right, and my mom said, 'We're leaving.' And I said, 'Is Daddy coming?' And she said, 'No.'

"I crumbled in that moment. It's the saddest memory I have. And my dad got down on his knees and hugged me and cried." Wendy begins crying again as she spoke. "I didn't see him for a long time. When Mom left he got depressed. He couldn't eat and lost 40 pounds.

"I saw him very little after that. My mom and I moved into a commune with the man who was to become my stepfather, in Mill Valley. It was a very small commune, basically just a bunch of hippies who decided to live in a big house together.

"When I was with my dad, I was happy. I just loved him. And he did not always show up after that as the responsible parent. There were times between eight and ten where my dad was supposed to be on schedule to take me for the weekend. Mom said it would break her heart—I would pack my little bag and get all ready and he wouldn't come. He'd call on the phone and say, 'I'm on call.'

"I don't think he understood how crazy I was about him, how much I needed him. They were very young when they had me. When I was eight, my dad was 29. And probably an emotionally stunted 29 because he'd spent his whole life being a cerebral guy. So now he was often meeting women and doing stuff and being social. And I was so funny; he would bring me back after a weekend and he'd drive away and I'd cry because I was so worried that he would be lonely without me. I'd watch him drive away by himself and think, 'What will he do?

That's so sad, he's gonna be so lonely without me.'

"In some ways this sort of unavailability of my dad for some years colored who I chose to date. I did tend toward people who were unavailable. I think that's beginning to change. The last five years I seem to only attract men who are extremely needy, which also isn't working out, but closer in the right direction."

Wendy moved back in with her father during high school. As they resumed their relationship, anger replaced her innocent infatuation. "I was mad at him all the time. I was mad at him because I had to leave all my friends to come live with him. My mom was in Marin, so moving from there to the East Bay might as well be another state. It was ultimately my parents' choice that I lived with him. My dad really wanted to know what it was like to have me as a daughter before I left home. And things weren't going well with my mom and my step-dad, so she was good with that.

"I was pretty mean to him. And one day I walked into his office and I saw this stack of four or five books on his desk: How to be a good father, How to talk to your teenager, all these self-help books. Then I thought, 'I gotta take it easy on him.' Seeing those books...I was touched by that. As young and selfish as teenagers can be, I looked at that and I thought, 'Wow, he's trying.' I was touched by the vulnerability."

Thirty years later, Wendy and her father are close. She's now a full-time nursing student, and he's paying her tuition. They talk several times a week on the phone.

"I have a 4.0. It's turned out that I have some aptitude that I think never really was available because I had no drive. I didn't care. My dad and I talked about it, and I said it's like a whole other person I didn't know existed. This whole school-student thing, this whole brain thing, that wasn't where we connected for all of my life until just recently.

"I really like the way that my father moves through the world, in a way that's intelligent and kind and diplomatic. I learned that from him. My father's warm and sweet and I think those parts of me came from him."

I asked Wendy what else she learned from her father, and how. "I remember doing something nice for someone that I didn't really want to be doing, so I was moaning about it, and I remember my dad saying, 'Here's the thing about that: If you're going to do something nice for somebody, do it with good humor. Because otherwise all the goodness gets lost. Get over your resentment.'

"I think my dad does the right thing, the responsible thing, always. And I'm like a person that people want to leave their kids with. I'm the person people want to be the godparent. I'm willing to behave with the best interests of others in mind. I think I learned that from my dad. That's not hard for me; in fact, what's hard for me is to understand why other people don't do that.

"I'm very intuitive. Part of the work I did in LA was intuitive counseling. I think any intuitive gifts I have come from my dad, who's very intuitive. He's got a good heart. And as a result, I have a good heart. That's a thing I often hear, and I think I got that from my dad.

"There are lots of stories where my dad hurt my feelings, or didn't show up, or disappointed me as a parent. It's just that overall I think he's so great, and I'm so grateful for him. And I think if anything the hard part about my dad is that I love him so much and in some ways he'll always be a little less available to me than I am to him. Because that's who he is. But I know, and my mom always says this, 'Your father is crazy about you.' I'm sure that's true. He tells me all the time how proud he is of me, how much he loves me, what a great person he thinks I am. He tells me good stuff all the time. He's been a great father, really."

Scientist's Daughter

I met Cheryl Berglund Coupé in 1998, and our paths crossed in professional circles frequently after that. Born in Canada, she was in her late forties when we met for our interview.

Cheryl's father Neil was born in Ignace, a small town in north-western Ontario. He grew up exploring the woods and taking tourists on hunting and fishing trips.

Neil went on to earn a master's degree in engineering from MIT. Cheryl learned to walk on the plane her family took to Stanford, where her father had been admitted for his PhD. That was a metaphor for much of her life to come, as she continues to walk in his footsteps.

When Cheryl was two, her father went to work at Bell Labs in Murray Hill, New Jersey. "It was just an absolute think tank," she said. "I mean it was the geekiest scientists in the world. Right up until high school, we would watch filmstrips in science class and it was in labs that I had gone to with my dad.

"Dad and I had a wonderful relationship. I do with both my parents. But I very definitely had a thing, one of those stereotypical, father-daughter hero kind of relationships. And he was doing cool stuff. I was, I guess, raised by a geek so I thought geeky stuff was cool."

When Cheryl was twelve, her father attended a scientific conference at a resort in Florida and brought his family. Cheryl's mother became ill and could not attend the opening reception, so Cheryl went instead. The next summer, Neil took her to a conference he was leading in Maine. During her senior year in college, Neil introduced her to a colleague at Intel, and Cheryl worked there for a semester. So began her career in high technology, which evolved into a career as a technology marketing writer and later as an author.

I was enamored with the lessons Cheryl took from her father and that she shared. "He talks about never closing doors, ever. You keep as many options open as long as you possibly can. And then the big thing is you make a decision with the best information you have, and you never look back. That's a huge one, that's from as far back as I can remember. You make the best decision you can, and then you never look back—'We should never have moved here'—sort of thing. We don't think that way. 'Here's why we did it, these are all the reasons.' Probably a very scientific approach.

"There is a certain freedom in saying 'never look back.' You make a decision and go forward, because it was the best decision you could make at the time. That is enormously freeing. So as I've made decisions through my career and with my husband and my family and things, there is nothing that I can look back at and say, 'You know, I should not have done that, I should have done something different, I should have made a different choice,' because that's just not the way I think.

"And then, sort of this half-joking thing, he always talked about Berglund (his family name) luck. We had sort of a joke thing, that Dad would always get in the toll booth line that would go through fastest, but it was sort of living your life so that you were there to take advantage of that luck. You know, that you had to do the right things, you had to make the right choices, and then the luck would find you. Those are the kind of things we talk to our kids about, too. What is it that you can do that continues to get you closer to where you want to be but doesn't shut any other doors?

"The other thing is a complete, complete focus on family, absolutely dedicated to family. Dad has lots of friends, he does a lot of things socially, but he truly would be perfectly happy with just my mom and family. So we tend to be very focused on family as well."

I wondered if her father felt career pressures as a highly accomplished scientist from Stanford and how he balanced his work and family life.

"The career was important to him, and certainly it feels good to have that accomplishment and there's certainly pride in that, but it was something for his family. That was the number one thing in his life always. I remember from the time I was a kid we had breakfast with my dad before going to school. He was almost always there. He traveled and things, but he was there for dinner, he was there for us, he was there at concerts, that was the important thing."

Cheryl's father shaped her understanding of her place as a woman in the world. She grew up around scientists, so why would she ever question her place among them as an adult?

"Professionally, it never occurred to me that there was anything that wasn't open to me," she said. "I spent my career as a young woman in a very old-boys world. I started out in test and measurement, for God's sake. It doesn't get any more old-boy than that. And I was a senior buyer at a tech company when I was 24, and I fought for that.

"I had been an assistant buyer and they had a senior buyer position open and I said, 'Wait a minute, I'm looking at the job description and I do all of this, why don't I have that job?' And they said, 'Oh, well, it says right here you have to have five years' experience.' And I said, 'Well, just because it takes somebody else five years to get to the point where they can do this job, why should I be penalized? I'm already doing this job.'"

Cheryl's story was another one that helped me see the importance of a father bringing masculine energy to his daughter. Unconsciously, I'd always assumed that girls learn how to be women from their mothers, and then by other significant women in their lives. I was operating under a set of conventional yet outdated beliefs. This was an enormous revelation to me, that girls learn how to become women from their fathers, not just their mothers. I was coming to see and hear that in rich detail.

As I talked with Cheryl and other women, I came to see how every woman takes in some dose of feminine and masculine—or the more gender-neutral yin and yang—energy from each parent. Those women who'd broken through gender barriers in the workplace, sports, and elsewhere during recent decades did so in no small part because of the masculine energy their fathers infused. Yet I hadn't ever appreciated that this was part of my role.

I saw in Cheryl and other women who drew the long straw that masculinity and femininity aren't opposites; they're intertwined. I came to see, over time, how some of the healthiest men I know are "Masculine-feminine" and how the healthiest women I know are "Feminine-masculine."

This was among my greatest realizations to come from these conversations. I've come to believe that a big part of my work as a father is to fill the alpha-energy tank that each of my daughters was born with.

Daughters need their masculinity now more than ever, as the glass ceilings of a male-dominated world continue to crack and open new opportunities for women. In education, for example, women in the US now receive more doctoral, Master of Arts, and Bachelor of Arts degrees than men. Young, single, childless women living in US cities earn eight percent more than their male counterparts, according to the US Census Bureau. Why? They're more highly educated.

But simply getting a superior education, or a career head start, doesn't guarantee a woman's success. Most of the world's cultures are still patriarchal. So are most complex organizations of business, education, government, and religion. Daughters need to be able to defend and assert themselves in this world to reach their full potential and rightful place.

Sometimes women will need to open doors to their futures with finesse, and sometimes they'll need to kick them down, as Cheryl did early in her career. She had internalized her father's composure and confidence after years of attending scientific conferences and research labs with him. When some corporate bureaucrat told her she didn't have the experience for the senior buyer's job she wanted, Cheryl knew just where she stood.

"I fought for the job and I got it," she said, "so from that standpoint, professionally it never occurred to me that there were things that I could not do."

Jews Don't Work for Other People

Elizabeth found out about my work through a relative, and wanted to have a conversation with me about her father. She was born in Philadelphia in 1945. Her father, of Russian ancestry, passed on countless lessons to his daughter—not only about money, but about the things in life that matter more than that.

"Dad did everything on his own," Elizabeth told me as we talked about his history. "He was a totally self-made person. He went through high school but he never went to college. He stayed in Philadelphia, and he met my mother in Wildwood, on a beach. They eloped when Dad was 25 and Mom was seventeen, and then moved to Florida with no money.

"Dad became a milkman on a horse and cart. They stayed in Florida for a few years, then my mother, who was pregnant with my brother, wanted to go north to Philadelphia. So they moved up north and Dad opened a supermarket."

The food market on the University of Pennsylvania campus generated enough cash, Elizabeth said, that her parents were able to begin investing in real estate. Small investments led to larger ones. "They would buy buildings for cash," she said. "I still remember that.

If you didn't pay cash, you didn't buy it. Dad never financed anything in his whole life.

"I learned you don't charge it. That has endured with me 100 percent for my entire life. I never thought of doing anything without buying the whole bloody thing. When I did have a lot of money, before the market crash and someone stealing many millions from me, I called up my stockbroker one day because I needed a new car. And I wouldn't buy the car I wanted unless there was enough in dividends. I needed $75,000. But if I didn't have dividends for $75,000 I wouldn't buy it. And the broker laughed at me and said, 'You can go buy whatever you want to buy.'

"But that's always been where my mind is. I never touched the principal, even when I inherited it. It was my money, but it was very hard for me to use it. I bought my houses, two of them, for cash. That's what Dad said. And these were very nice houses."

Her parents' growing real estate income led to investments in the stock market. "Dad was brilliant in the market," Elizabeth said. "When we were very young, he taught us how to read the buy/sell columns in the business section of the paper. For my birthday, and my brother's birthday, we'd get stock. So we could watch our stock, and from our allowance we were to buy stock. And then we'd learn how you could lose all your money in something if your stock tanked. That happened."

The family's growing wealth led her parents to focus on what mattered most to them—sharing it, educating their children, and giving them a place in the world they'd never had.

"My mother was the founder of a Jewish orphanage," Elizabeth continued. "On Passover, she would invite the majority of the orphans to our house and we'd have this huge Seder. And my father supported all of this. He just was a really good person. Down to earth. Low key. Very religious. I miss him at every Seder. He was always there for me. He was never too busy working.

"Dad was a sports fanatic. He and I had season tickets to every sporting event in Philadelphia. We saw the Eagles, the Phillies, the 76ers. We went to all the home games. All of them! It was a very big part of my life, sports. I loved sports. I started going with him maybe when I was seven or eight, until I left for college at seventeen. Dad always taught me I could do whatever I wanted to do. Whatever your goal is, you can do it if you're qualified. Don't let sexism or religion ever stand in your way."

Elizabeth received a bachelor of fine arts degree from the University of Pennsylvania, then studied at the University of Poitiers in Tours, France. After that she moved to New York and worked as an art director at a large Madison Avenue advertising firm, an unusual position for a woman in the 1960s. In that patriarchal world of drugs, booze, and hypocrisy, the principles she absorbed from her father kept her grounded.

"Dad always taught me, 'Your ideals and your morals are more important than anything else.' I once had a confrontation with a boss who wanted me to be somewhere on Yom Kippur. I remember looking at this guy, the CEO of the agency, and saying, 'No, it's my holiday.' And he looked at me and said, 'If you don't go, you're fired.' And I said, 'Then I'm fired. My integrity means more to me than you do or the job.'

"I didn't go to the meeting. And he didn't fire me. And I really laid down my own laws then. I left there after two years; I didn't like the scene. Dad taught me that you never sell yourself short. You never sell your *self*. He was a phenomenal role model. And I took so much from him.

"Dad was never pretentious. He always looked, and I'd laugh about it, kind of homeless. He would just put on clothes. And he was colorblind. So unless they were going to a black tie do, and Mom would put out a tux and shoes with the right color socks, he would look like a beggar. And he loved it."

Among Elizabeth's fondest memories of her father is his unwavering support. "I had a parakeet named Budgie. I must have been six when my bird died, and I was devastated. And I remember calling my dad at the store and he came home immediately. He was never too busy, no matter what he did in his life, if I needed him. Dad came home, and we packed up Budgie, and Dad was going to bury him. Dad took me to a pet store and bought me a new parakeet. He was there for me, no matter what.

"I adored him. He was smart, funny, loved me to bits, was very expressive in a healthy way. Dad would encourage me in whatever mediums I needed from the time I was little. Sketch pads, crayons, it didn't matter. He just said to enjoy what I was doing. That's what I remember and that's how he lived his life for me. He cared for me my whole life. And I cared for him at the end of his life. He taught me to appreciate so much in the world and to take nothing for granted.

"I remember I had this beautiful ring they'd given me for my birthday, it had opals and diamonds. And I was washing my hands in New Orleans in a train station and the ring went down the drain. I remember going to a pay phone and calling Dad collect, crying about this ring. Dad said, 'Are your fingers okay?' And I said, 'What do you mean, are my fingers okay? My fingers are fine.'

'Are you okay?'

'I'm fine.'

And he said, 'It's only money. We'll buy you another ring. As long as you're okay, you didn't do it on purpose, things happen.' Those are the kind of lessons of judgment that Dad would instill in me that I instilled in my children.

"As an example, my little one was practicing soccer at our house and she broke the garage windows kicking the soccer ball. She came in and said, 'You're gonna kill me.' I said, 'Did you get hurt?'

'No.'

'Did you do it on purpose?'

'No.'

'Then there's nothing to worry about. You didn't get hurt, you didn't do it maliciously. Next time I won't give you the idea to kick against the garage door'."

Having money was important to Elizabeth's father, for the freedom it could buy his family. But he clearly didn't care about appearing to have money.

"My father was frugal. He never lived lavishly. Dad would buy station wagons, but because he was color blind, he would come home and say, 'I just bought a green station wagon,' and we'd go outside and it would be Smurf blue. He didn't care. He always bought something very American, General Motors or something, and they were really ugly. And Dad would keep them.

"Once Dad and I were at a ball game, and I must have been ten. There was a long tractor trailer and it had metal pilings on it and Dad backed right into it and the pilings came through the back of the station wagon. And all Dad cared about was if we were all right. He never cared when his cars got ruined or dented.

"I remember Dad taking this car in, and they straightened the frame and replaced everything. But they didn't do a good job on the paint. And instead of Dad sending it back, he got paint and a roller. I'll never forget it, Dutch Boy Green. He went out to the driveway. He rolled paint on the car. And the gardener was there doing the lawn, so the car had grass fibers on it! Dad didn't care. It didn't bother him. He was unique. He was never preoccupied with the appearance of things, with how wealthy he appeared."

In her family, Elizabeth recalled, she was taught, "You don't work for other people. When you're Jewish, you work for yourself. My friends' parents all worked for themselves. I didn't know anyone who worked for somebody else. They all had their own companies, their own thing that they started. None of these men had educations, or the women, they were first generation Americans. And when my first daughter got one of her jobs, I made the inane comment of, 'Jews don't do that, you don't work for other people.' And I meant it, because that's what was instilled with me. I worked for someone else maybe twice in my life and that's it."

As her father entered the closing chapters of his life, Elizabeth began taking care of him. "Once I had children, the kids and I flew down to Florida for every single Jewish holiday. When Dad got ill, I went down, I took care of him, got help. There was nothing I wouldn't do for Dad. He had a stroke in the afternoon, he had a heart attack that night, and he held on until I got there. He died in my arms. He knew I was there."

In my interviews I asked the women I met with what they didn't get from their fathers, if anything, that they longed for in retrospect. Elizabeth had an immediate and unequivocal answer to that question. "Nothing. Zero regrets. He didn't miss anything. I'm a very lucky person."

She cried as she recalled her first two marriages, how her husbands died, and how neither had her father's qualities. Elizabeth recently married for the third time. "It took me 63 years to find a man equal to my dad. Bryan has all of these incredible virtues and qualities. He is just that good. My dad would adore him. And there's no greater joy for me than knowing that. That makes my eyes tear. That I could say, 'Hey, Dad! I got it right.' I'm a very lucky woman.

"In the Jewish religion, when someone dies, there's no higher honor than burying the person yourself. I had seen that done at someone's funeral and I asked Dad about it, and he said, 'It's the highest honor.' And I said, 'Dad, the girls and I will do that for you.'

"At my dad's funeral, my brother and the rabbi wanted to leave and have the help do it. I told the rabbi he and the help could leave, that the girls and I would bury Dad to honor him. The rabbi said to me, 'No, you cannot!' And I said to him, 'You will get hit by my shovel if you don't move.' It was that important to me."

I don't know many women who have zero regrets about their fathers. Elizabeth's was one of those stories, like many of those shared so far in this book, that I didn't see examples of when I read through some of the published works on fathers and daughters and the dysfunctional nature of those relationships.

Elizabeth's dad was a hero. He loved her, she loved him. He went from milkman to millionaire, and yet he never lost his sense of who he was. And he never seemed to lose sight of the importance of the small things that make the big difference, like taking his daughter to sporting events and coming home from work when her pet parakeet died.

Elizabeth was with her father when he died, and with him when he was buried. She made sure of that. I can't think of any higher honor, either, than how he left this world—buried by his daughter who wouldn't take no for an answer.

Pushing the
Boundaries

I met Amy Sibal when I was in my late forties and she was in her early thirties. We were at a seminar together, offered by a gifted man whom I consider one of my teachers. Amy has an interesting combination of intelligence, sass, playfulness, and social consciousness. A physicist by training, she was 38 and single at the time of our conversation and was working as a middle school teacher.

Amy's father was seven when he lost his own father—a Czechoslovakian immigrant—to cancer. Her father studied engineering at Rutgers, where he met his future wife. He was there in ROTC "basically to pay for his education," Amy said, when he got orders to go to Germany. So he proposed to the woman who became his wife.

"It wasn't like this romantic thing," Amy continued. "It was much more practical. They loved each other, but it was like, 'I have to go to Germany for two years, you want to come? And if you want to come, we have to get married.' And my mom was like, 'Okay!'"

Born in New Jersey after her parents returned, Amy grew up pushing boundaries, but she always found in her father the stability she needed. Hers was one of the many stories I heard from women who grew up with tough love from their fathers.

"I can remember always totally being my dad's little girl. He picked me up a lot, and he was the kind of person who let me jump on him. I said 'Daddy' before 'Mommy;' I hear about that all the time. And my mom tells me that when my father was present I was just ecstatic.

"I remember the day my sister was born, when I was about two and a half. All of a sudden people came in the house, they took me to the neighbors. I remember wondering after an hour or two, 'Where are my mom and dad?' and not understanding what was going on. And I remember my dad all of a sudden knocking on the screen door and seeing him and I was just so excited. He was below the porch and I ran and just jumped at him. I was so happy that he was there.

"My father was always so loving, so I remember that feeling, my first vivid memory. I remember just being like, 'Dad's here!' and being so happy that finally he was here and to see his smile. And I remember just holding onto him and him giving me a big hug, telling me, 'It's fine, your mom's fine, everything's fine, and we'll take you to your grandmother's.' That's kind of the role he always played with me. He was always the stabilizer.

"When we were children, he was definitely affectionate. He held us napping on him, even probably up until we were five or six. I remember being little enough to fall asleep on his chest."

As Amy was growing up, her father worked in New York City as a civil engineer for Western Electric, then for AT&T. She fondly recalled her father's support as she became involved in sports and later struggled in school.

"When I was about three years old, my dad would be outside pulling me around on skis on little moguls that he'd made. We would go skiing every year and swimming. I was a high jumper, I ran, I was a basketball player, a gymnast, I swam, I played soccer, I dove, and pretty much any sport I did he was there. I didn't play a lot and he was always supportive of showing up to the games and being there.

"I can remember if I was really nervous, my dad would stand behind me with his arm on my shoulder right before I'd compete. I could have never asked for a person to be more supportive of anything in my life. He was a very significant family figure, he was home every night at a certain point, sat down, had dinner at six.

"My father was very into our education. If he'd see problems, we were going to get tutored somewhere after school, to make sure that we were comfortable. Word problems were hard for me, but I was amazing at math. So when I was in sixth, maybe seventh grade, I used to come home and my father would write two word problems for me every night that I'd have to do to just train my brain. For like two years. And then it wasn't a problem anymore. I got really good at them, obviously, because I'm a physicist now and it's basically all about extracting information and putting it into math. He was very supportive of pretty much everything that I tried.

"Everybody liked my father. He was one of those kind of people. He was stern and he got done what needed to be done, but I always heard wonderful things. We'd go up for the Christmas parties, or when he'd have colleagues over for dinner, I was always hearing about, 'Oh, your father's amazing.' So it was very interesting to realize as I got older, 'Wow! My dad does all this stuff!' Because to me he was just my father.

"One of his big things he was known for was making sure that the women engineers were moving forward in the company, getting the promotions they needed. He was the one the women went to if they felt that they were getting slighted. A lot of us cousins are girls, and my grandfather and father were pretty much like, 'You guys can do anything men can do, and even better. Don't ever think any different.' My father's attitude all my life was, 'You're a girl, but you can do everything a boy can do and then some.'

"I was the tomboy. I was the one who had the skirt with the tube socks on and my mother and my aunt would give me shit, and my dad would say, 'Leave her alone!' He was always supportive of whatever outfit I would come down with. My mom would be like, 'Could you go upstairs and take the tube socks off or brush your hair?' And Dad would say, 'What's wrong with her?'

"In that way, he was kind of my cheerleader. We all have our ideas of how people should be dressing and looking and my father was always very supportive coming from a family that would have liked me to be a little more prim and proper and dressing accordingly. My father was like, 'Whatever. Don't listen to them. You're fine.' So he definitely supported the rebellious aspect in me.

"I remember my first period. I was supposed to go to the beach for my birthday and I got my period and I didn't want to go. And my dad looked at me and I was trying to tell him this but it was so embarrassing. 'Dad, I just don't think we should go.' My father's like, 'I don't get this. What is going on?'

"And my mom said, 'Okay, if she's not going to tell you, I will. She's got her period.' And he was like, 'Aren't there those things you just stick up you? You're going to have to learn how to do it anyway. Get upstairs and go to it.' And my mom's like, 'You mean the tampon?' And he's like, 'Yeah. Go show her how to do that. We're going to the beach. It's her birthday, she's going with all her friends, there's no reason why her period should stop it.'"

The "tough" half of the tough love Amy received came mostly from her father. "My mother was the worrier and my father was the disciplinarian. My mother never, ever disciplined. So if we got in trouble, it would be like, 'Wait until your father gets home.' And my father had the voice, like, people heard him up at the end of the street.

"I was spanked once, when I was four or five. I think it was one of the times I'd done something and my mom was like, 'You wait till your father gets home.' And my father got home and he was like, 'Get over here.' I remember trying to put a book down my pants, and my dad said, 'Don't play me for a fool.' And he gave me a good spanking. And once in high school when I called my mom a bitch at the kitchen table I got it across the back of the head so hard that my head rung for a day or two. The response time was so quick that you would have been amazed.

"I've always been a boundary pusher. And you don't call your mother that, so I'm glad for what happened, because it forced me to check in. I don't think that anything would have resonated with me as strongly as that response. It was an instant response, it was at that core level like *not okay*. I think, if he'd yelled at me or something, I wouldn't have probably remembered that. I probably would have done it again.

"My mother has some up and down issues and it's always amazed me how he's always stayed on an even keel all the time, even when my mom was flipping out. You always knew, even if things were getting out of control, he would pull it in line. He would put the boundaries out there, and I think we knew that. So even if my mom was acting really irrational about something, we knew when Dad came home, everything would be fine.

"Definitely my father was the shit to me as I grew up. I looked to him for the stability and for direction. The support came from both of them but he was definitely the one that was driving. Driving it but also that was what I was craving more. I needed to see him being proud, I wanted to see him being supportive. It was great if my mom did it, but he was the one I was looking for. I wanted Dad there.

'My father was very sensitive, but also the stern one. He was very loving, very caring. He never tried to fix people, but he was always there. I think he basically made sure he played that role that he felt he never had.'"

Amy's story was one more nail in the coffin of the father I used to be. Daughters, especially "spirited" daughters like Amy and my own, need the toughness of their fathers as much as they need their love. In fact, I've changed my entire notion of what parental "love" is. I think it's both tender and firm. It's about boundaries as much as it is about bonding. And with the "long straw" interviews I did, I came to see so much of what I had failed to provide my daughters with. I had shied away from the full weight of authority that my daughters needed from me. I think it was because of my own upbringing in an authoritarian environment.

I realize so much more clearly now how children need sensitivity and compassion, but that they also need stability, direction, and a clear sense that their parents are in charge. They need a strong presence from their fathers; they need to feel the force of his masculinity. And I was coming to see that I'd failed by letting the pendulum swing too far in the direction of leniency masquerading as sensitivity. I came to the point in this work where I realized that I'd only delivered on half of the tough-love equation, and it was the easy half.

Authentic Actress

Mariah Castle was the youngest woman I met with during my interviews. At 28, she had acted in film, theater, and commercials, and for about eighteen months prior to our meeting she had been the bride in the San Francisco production of "Tony and Tina's Wedding," an interactive play that's been staged in several US cities. She also teaches acting.

Mariah's father Duke, the first of three children, was born near Chicago in 1943 and took from his mother a strong faith in Christian Science. He grew up with an affinity for electronics and building things such as the crystal radio he created from scratch, which foreshadowed the career ahead of him.

Despite being the youngest woman I interviewed, Mariah had an unusually intimate understanding of her father. She knew a number of stories about his growing up, such as when he got a BB gun for his birthday and shot a bird. "He killed the bird and he was just devastated and was like, 'I will never kill anything again.' He didn't want to see his gun anymore and he didn't want to ever cause harm to another living being. That's been a strong influence in his life and in mine as well."

What struck me in particular was how much she knew of her father's experiences of failure and rejection, and the authentic quality of their relationship that his openness engendered. This is much like the relationship that Kim, who grew up in a boy's body, experienced with her father, and her conclusion that "the only way he can know me is if I trust and I share." In Mariah's case, it was her father who opened the door of self-disclosure, which allowed his daughter to come to know him as not just her father but as a man—with all of the successes and failures, joys and pain that we all experience as fathers but usually hide behind the facades we present to the world.

"My mom and aunts told me as I was growing up that my dad is a very sensitive, kind, and gentle man, who has a really good balance of masculine and feminine within himself. So he's not a real guy's guy. He can keep up with the guys. He can talk and enjoy sports and barbecue and all that. But I never felt this overwhelming dose of masculinity or testosterone in the house.

"He's always been a sensitive male. He had strong friendships. But every so often, he would come up against big moments of rejection, like once being told in high school he had to leave this trio he was in because they didn't think he was good enough. That was really crushing to him. But the way he tells it, any big life obstacle he's come up against, or any period of rejection, has opened the door to something better and greater. That's a huge life lesson he's tried to teach me.

"He went to Cornell University, and had a bit of a rough start. He wanted to be in a fraternity, but didn't get asked to pledge any of them. And that was really crushing. He ended up talking to an older student, a friend of the family, who talked to the fraternity my dad liked best and said, 'Give this guy a chance. He might not make the best first impression, but he's a good person and you'll be glad to have him in your house.' So he was in that fraternity and loved it. That was a defining experience in his college years, along with academics. He was disciplined and achieved highly as an electrical engineering student.

"After college, he got his MBA at Stanford. Prestigious colleges have been a defining part of his life, and that's impacted me as well, the status of that education."

Duke met his first wife in California. They married shortly after he finished graduate school and lived in California for about ten years while he worked as an engineer. As Mariah tells it, her father wasn't lacking for confidence professionally—until a harsh lesson in workplace realities hit him.

"He talks about how he felt like a real hotshot when he got out of school. He'd done really well in both undergrad and graduate school and felt like he was kind of the man and could do anything. Then he had a couple of reality checks, where he was let go from a job or two. But again, he would say that opened up an opportunity for something better, and he ended up at Hewlett-Packard."

Her father's openness was a gift to Mariah—literally. "He wrote out a chronicle of his biggest moments of rejection throughout the stages of his life and how they taught him a lesson. He gave it to me as a gift when I broke up with my very first boyfriend who was the big love of my life when I was in my early twenties. I had a really hard time finding my way out of that breakup. And the main thing he offered me was that whenever something terrible happens, it's almost always making space for something unimaginably better to happen—the largest case in point being his first wife divorcing him made space for him to meet my mom and have me.

"He didn't see it coming and was completely crushed and shocked," Mariah said of the divorce. "That's probably the biggest grieving experience of his life.

"It was really difficult for him to lose everything and start over at ground zero, not knowing what was going on with his life or what he was destined for, and really sad to lose both of the kids in addition to losing his wife.

"He got engaged eventually to another woman, and says their relationship was a lot of fun. Before they got married, two of Dad's best friends found out she was having an affair, and they told her either she could tell Dad or they would. He had actually already guessed it, and again, he was devastated.

"So after that, he decided to just get out there and meet a bunch of people and really explore. He went on something like 50 dates and really enjoyed meeting a lot of people. Nothing serious came of that, until his last date turned out to be my mom. They were both part of a spiritual organization called Creative Initiative, sort of a Christian group that would now be kind of New Age-y. So they have always had a spiritual foundation in their relationship."

Two years later, Mariah was born. And shortly after that, her father left the security of his job at H-P. He spent eighteen months exploring his options before deciding to start a marketing consulting business. Among the challenges that tested his faith was coming to accept that the money would always come in when it was needed.

"Dad didn't have a reliable salary, so he worried about money over the years. I never felt like we didn't have enough, but I never felt like we had a lot to spend, though I realize now we lived a pretty affluent life. My mom never worked after I was born. And Dad had to learn to trust that the work would always come, because it always did, even when it would get absolutely down to the wire and he would think, 'How am I going to make it through the rest of the month?'

"He tells a story of one time things were getting incredibly tight and he was really worried. And some money from his stocks just showed up at the front door, like $20,000. It happens like that all the time for him, and it's a lesson he keeps having to learn. He's tried to teach me that as well—if you're following your heart and being responsible with your money, no matter how unsecure it might seem at times, it always works out—the money will always be there, the universe is providing for you—and to trust in the universe financially, emotionally, everything in life.

"He was there in the evenings and on the weekends. And he likes a lot of quiet time and private time to read and just do whatever he does. But he would come out and play and we'd always have meals together, dinner and breakfast on the weekends. He would take me out to breakfast sometimes. Going to get doughnuts on a Sunday was so special and exciting. Or going to McDonalds for breakfast."

That physical play of her childhood years began to fade as Mariah matured, and she found herself longing for more physical affection from her father. "We always hug when we greet each other and when we leave. But my dad always seems uncomfortable saying, 'I love you.' And there wasn't a lot of physical contact when I was little. He's so great at relating on an intellectual and philosophical level, and the calm, quiet presence of him is always there. But when it comes to physical intimacy, it's not as frequent.

"When I was in my teens and early twenties, I saw a spiritual teacher. And she said there was a physical distance between my dad and me, a lack of physical connection. She said I should ask him to be more physically affectionate. And I did not want to do that. But she kept bringing it up. So eventually, I sat my dad down. I could hardly look at him. And I told him, 'I feel like we have a little bit of physical disconnect between us, and I just want you to know that I would like you to be more physically affectionate towards me.' I think it made him really uncomfortable, but he's made more of an effort ever since."

That desire continues as a theme in her adult life. "I'm always wanting more physical affection from the men I'm attracted to. They do give a good amount, but I have this unquenchable thirst for it. I've actually had very few serious partnerships. That first one was a huge deal.

"Since then, I haven't had what I would call a serious boyfriend that lasted more than four months. That's been the challenge of my twenties, why am I single and why can't I find somebody that I really want to be with. I think part of it is because the relationship I was born from is so unusual and had this intense way that it happened and this spiritual foundation. It's unique, their relationship and the way they brought me up. I'm probably subconsciously looking for something that amazing and not finding it."

Mariah's openness helped me enormously in my understanding of women, desire, and intimacy. Her father provided for her financially; he gave her his attention and time while she was growing up. And yet with all of that remarkable parenting, she could still clearly feel her need for physical affection and intimacy that hadn't been fully met.

I saw in Mariah and other women how their intimate relationships with men are so intricately connected to the relationships with their fathers. Feeling attractive and interesting to the first man in their lives—and finding acceptance, playfulness, and physical affection—makes an enormous difference for daughters as they come into relationships with men later in their lives.

End of the Rainbow

I knew Ruth Burk as a professional acquaintance. She's a business writer with a boutique consulting firm. I heard her talk once about how she looks forward to going on vacation every year with her father, and how much she loves his company. So when I thought of women to interview for this book, I wanted to hear her story. "How," I wondered, "does a father make *that* happen?"

When we met a few months later for our interview, I actually found myself feeling envious as our time together passed. At 41 years of age she was remarkably content. The humble and loving father inside of her helped Ruth find what so many of us are consumed with pursuing, often down the wrong paths—peace of mind and a life of abundance.

Ruth's father was born in 1929, the third son of German immigrants. He married his best friend's younger sister, and has been married for more than 50 years.

"My dad got a job for the Highway Department and worked there for over 30 years," she told me. "He drove like a million miles all over the state. He knows every back road, every best place to have a picnic on any highway or byway.

"A lot of my memories are with my family and my dad. We had two and a half acres, and spent a lot of time outside running around.

I remember Dad would get home right around five o'clock every day. He had a huge garden, half an acre, rows and rows of corn and beans and everything. In the summertime he would come in, change his clothes, and go out to the garden and pick whatever we were going to eat for dinner that night.

"We also did a lot of bike riding as a family, and my mom and dad would both go riding with us around the neighborhoods. One of my fondest memories of my dad was playing catch with him in the side yard, just throwing the ball back and forth. He'd do it with my brothers and with me, just one on one. And that was cool, because we had his undivided attention.

"He helped us make forts, multi-story forts, and they were great. Like seven levels. Even by today's standards, they were pretty extravagant tree houses. We had chickens and we always had goofy animals—turkeys, rabbits, and stuff around.

"He read at night to us. That was a big thing he did with us. I remember sitting on my dad's lap. One time I climbed up and got settled in and cracked his rib. He was always a big passionate reader so I saw that modeled all the time. I'm a huge reader and so is my husband, and our kids are.

"And camping, that's another big memory. Friday at five o'clock, my mom would have the Volkswagen van and a tent trailer all packed. We'd just camp over the weekend. We played basketball—we had an in-ground hoop, cemented in. I played on a boys' team in middle school."

When I asked Ruth what she remembered feeling about her father as she was growing up, she answered without hesitation. "I loved my dad, and he loved me. I just always wanted to do things with him, I wanted his attention, just like I wanted my mom's attention, but I never felt like I was in his way or he didn't have time for me."

Her father helped provide Ruth with something every child needs, and yet so few get enough of: Instruction, in the things that matter. "We were a good Methodist, church-going family," she said. "To this day my whole family still has a very strong belief in God and in faith. We all still identify as Christians; it's a big part of who we are. I was very involved in my church.

"He was very attentive to my schoolwork. From the very youngest years that I can look back on, when it came to education, my dad was always there for us. He helped me write my first report, in fourth grade, on chickens. He said, 'Ruth, I want you to learn how to research, how to write a good research report. So I will help you through every step of this process.'

"In high school my studies always came first. I always had to stay up on my homework. If my grades ever slid from a 4.0, if I ever got a B, we'd have a talk. I remember doing multiple hours of homework a night, sitting down at the kitchen table, and if I had questions I would go to him. He was there every evening if we needed him. He was just always real supportive of anything I wanted to do.

"I went out for gymnastics one year, and I played basketball. In high school, my focus was on my studies and he encouraged that and he always said, 'Ruth, remember that no matter what else you do when you go to college, your studies come first.' And I would repeat that mantra to myself over and over. And it helped me out with parties, my social life. I always attended to my studies. That was because education was so important to him.

"My dad taught me to be very independent. I saw him do things; having your priorities straight, being true to yourself. My dad does not care what anybody else thinks of him. He's a good man and people like him. He is the craziest dresser. He wears hand-me-downs from my brothers and my husband. If I give him a shirt, he's like, 'What do I need this for?' He's got polyester pants from the '70s and '80s that he still wears. He just doesn't care.

"But he's very self-assured. We give him a hard time because even at Black Butte Ranch, where we have a second house, he'll ride his bike around in an orange jumpsuit. It looks like he's a jailbird. Being comfortable in your skin and not needing to pretend that you're anything that you aren't, I got that from him."

When Ruth was in fifth grade, her father declined a promotion because it would have meant uprooting the family from its church, schools, and community. "As an adult, I realize this is a man who had his priorities in order. It was more important for him to have his family life and to make the sacrifice with his career and to keep his family in one place where we were comfortable and happy."

Ruth now has a plot of land like the one she grew up on, with chickens and a garden. She lives 45 minutes from her father. "At Black Butte in the summer, he'll go on walks with us. He'll watch the kids if we want to go somewhere. He's just fun to have around. I look forward to that time with him. I like talking with him, relaxing with him, he's part of our routine there. It wouldn't be the same without him.

"I love my dad! I don't think I could have asked for anything more in the way of support, whether it was emotional or financial or whatever. The security that he has given me made me who I am today. He's a man of simple means. I have no regrets about my relationship with my dad. I love him and know he loves me."

I was struck by Ruth's rich family life, her father's sense of work-life balance, and the adult relationship they share. Her life is such a success story. She has found an abundance that money cannot buy. She has a life full of love, self-acceptance, and happiness.

Each of these women who drew the long straw, and the others whom I interviewed but could not include in this book, helped put a part of me to rest and let a new life come into being. I was humbled by their fathers' strength and dedication. Among the messages that stood out clearly was that great fathering has nothing to do with formal education, income, or professional status. The great dads I heard about, in the stories above and others, were a well-known scientist, a laborer, a garbage man, a bread truck driver, business managers, a highway department employee.

Being a great dad, I came to see clearly, is all about paying attention, showing up, showing and telling your daughter how much she means to you. It doesn't have anything to do with accomplishment, or the noise that many of us pursue in our search for personal significance.

The Long and the Short of It

> The pain of living with a father who just doesn't seem to care can be as devastating as outright desertion. An abandoned girl can console herself with fantasies that her far-away father really loves and misses her. But there is no dreaming away the daily, eyewitness evidence that a father cares more for his bottle or his book or his baseball game—or his son—than he does for his daughter.
>
> Barbara Goulter
> Joan Minninger, PhD
> *The Father-Daughter Dance*

As I was finishing this book, I attended a holiday concert put on by middle school and high school students. A high-school girl in the choir caught my attention during the performance. She towered over other girls around her. Her teeth were shackled with braces. And she was singing her heart out. She was alive in her music, and in that life was her absolute beauty.

As I sat and watched, I was overcome with questions: Does this girl have a father? As a lanky teenager in braces, did she have that safe relationship with the man she could trust, and did he tell her she was beautiful as she grew through that awkward period of her teens, and into the striking woman she was destined to become? I sat, thinking about this girl whose spirit and love for singing so clearly filled her with joy. Is she so full of life because she has a wonderful family and

73

a long-straw father? Or is she someone who finds singing so extraordinary because it transports her away from something else, like the things that I heard about repeatedly in my interviews that follow?

I sat there, holding on to the hope that she had someone who treasured her. Every day, about 200,000 daughters are born in the world.[1] Who among those daughters doesn't deserve to draw the long straw when it comes to her father? They all do. And yet only a few of them will be so blessed. Seeing this girl at the crucial inflection point in her life, between adolescence and womanhood, I was struck by the force of my questions about the father she might or might not have, and the role that he did or didn't play in her emergence. I wanted this girl, singing with so much joy and beauty, to be among the lucky few.

But even if she was, what about the other 199,999 daughters born on the same day? And every day? From everything I've come to see, most are not so lucky.

I spoke with many women whose fathers were somewhere in a gray zone between the heroic fathers of the previous section, and the horrific fathers that appear in "The Short Straw" section of this book.

"Between the long and the short of it," is what I call this gray zone. These women had fathers who were physically present but not emotionally engaged. Some of these men were ambivalent about their fathering responsibilities and generally neglectful of their daughters. Some women lost their fathers to divorce, death, or military duty, so on one hand they had fathers or had them for a while, but they missed something crucial as well.

These are women whose fathers were "there and not there." The resulting bond with their fathers is generally weaker than for those who drew the long straw. Fortunately, as the following stories show, these women have an easier time coming to terms with their pasts,

---

1 This is according to estimates from the US government and other bodies such as the United Nations.

and their fathers, than women whose relationships were more starkly painful.

Survivor

Airplanes and hotels are home for Jeanne Zucker. With nearly three million miles in one frequent flier account alone, she has, in her words, "seen just about everything you can see" on an airplane. This includes surprising an intimately-entangled couple in the airplane lavatory. She also curled up under blankets in the back row of a plane and slept through its landing at her destination and then its subsequent departure to Hawaii. She woke up halfway across the Pacific Ocean.

So I wasn't terribly surprised when she offered to fly to meet me for an interview.

Jeanne is a survivor, a woman who has navigated the male-dominated worlds of business and casinos. Her father is a survivor, too. He spent three years running from the Nazis in the 1940s, living under a barn and in a cave.

Born in Chicago in 1962, Jeanne grew up in New Jersey, attending public high school and Hebrew school at her synagogue. She was class valedictorian at both. She is a senior vice president with a health care technology company, and is on two boards of directors.

Jeanne attended Wellesley, and came out at night as a chain-laden member of the punk rock movement. She "experimented a lot… with all kinds of things" early in college, she said, yet did well enough to get into medical school. That lasted until she kept fainting at the sight of blood; she took her medical interests into health care business ventures. When she took a pay cut to get equity in a startup company, she wanted to make up for some of the lost income. So on Friday afternoons she headed out for poker weekends at a casino in Connecticut.

"I could navigate between two different worlds—a corporate world in my professional job and this black market, underworld casino life that I enjoyed on the weekend. The people were so interesting—mostly men, mostly very unhappy in their marriages, mostly coming to Foxwoods to escape, to feel empowered, to live a little bit on the edge in their own minds. I loved the lingo and the gossip and having to watch your back all the time, because you never knew what was going to happen next. And I loved being one of the very few women that was playing poker at that time.

"I did very well financially, because I had that intelligence and discipline and strong work ethic and endurance. I memorized stat tables and I developed a methodology for playing seven card stud and masked myself behind this exterior of 'Oh, she looks like a girl who could be my daughter; isn't that nice; we'll wipe her out.' And it would often turn on these gentlemen, because I was able to outsmart them very disarmingly. I loved those years, getting to know those people, know about their families. And where else could you be walking around at four in the morning with a wad of money in your pocket that you just picked up from a bunch of guys that were half-asleep and half-intoxicated?"

In her late forties when we met for our interview, Jeanne has never been married and has no children. "I likely will not have children, which I'm very comfortable with," she said. "I knew early on I had little to no interest in having children or having a family. I never felt that maternal instinct; I never felt that I had to nurture someone or be fulfilled by having a child."

This gambling, yet successful, single woman who's up in the air and not grounded in a family of her own has her psychological roots in a story that runs deep.

The eldest of two children, her father was born to a Jewish family in Wislica, Poland in 1922. His parents owned a dry goods store. He attended both the local Jewish school and the Polish public school system until 1939, when the war broke out. He was required to do forced labor, and had to drop out of school and help build a road between his town and another. By late 1942, as word came that Jews were being resettled to different areas of Poland, he grew increasingly suspicious of the Nazis.

"On the day that the deportation and the liquidation of Wislica took place, my father went into hiding with some of his cousins. My father's family had a hiding place in the house where they kept their money—mostly gold coins. He and his parents made an agreement that anyone who needed the money at any point during the war could go to that place, divide the money, and leave half there.

"His parents and his sister and all the other relatives and everyone else from the town participated in the resettlement. And, of course, we now know that they were not being resettled, but they were being deported. My father's entire family was taken to Treblinka. Very shortly after October 3rd, 1942, they were all murdered in Treblinka."

Her father and his cousins escaped capture by moving from town to town. They lived in a cave for part of the winter, until the snow put them at risk of being tracked whenever they ventured out. Jeanne's father went to a family that had frequented his family's store, and begged to be sheltered and hidden. Risking their lives, that family built a bunker beneath their horse stables, housing Jeanne's father and his cousins for 26 months. They lived in this hole, receiving potato soup and bread once or twice a day. Freedom came on January 13, 1945, when the Russians liberated Poland.

That year, her father went to Munich and, as part of the German government's reparations program, began his free education at the University of Munich.

"I've always taken a special interest in my father and his history, in part because it was a taboo subject when we were growing up. My father finally started talking about his experiences during the war after the movie *Schindler's List* came out. After that movie, survivors began to experience a bit of a celebrity status. It was kind of cool to be a survivor. He didn't have to be embarrassed. He didn't have to feel guilty that he survived. That movie for him was very liberating, and it represented closure with his family.

"After *Schindler's List* came out we did some things together which I would have never predicted. He began going to reunions with his classmates from the University of Munich—all of them survivors. They'd get together in Florida and the Catskills and talk about their experiences in Europe and their studies. I would go with him, and I was such an anomaly, because I was one of the few members of the second generation that would go to these things. And I was so enthralled by them, so fascinated by these people, because they were so tight and so fond of each other. You could tell they were almost like family to one another, because their families were all gone."

Her father came to the United States in 1950, and with his electrical engineering degree he worked as a TV repairman. Later he moved to Chicago and studied at the Illinois Institute of Technology, earning a PhD in electrical engineering. He married in 1961, and then accepted a job at Bell Laboratories in New Jersey in 1964.

"My father wanted to work for the premier engineering company at the time, which was Bell Laboratories, and that's what he was going to do. He was with Bell Laboratories for 35 years, retired there in a fairly senior position and now is still in New Jersey with my mom in the same house that I grew up in. He's still very mentally aware and acutely coherent. He's in really strong health, goes to the gym three times a week, and is just a great treasure in my life."

Jeanne and I went back into her earliest memories of her father, where she was in his life, and he in hers. "My fondest memories are when he and I would drive around together on Saturday and Sunday afternoons. And we would have no plan. We would just get in the car and drive for hours.

"It wasn't until many years later that I understood why my father liked to drive around without any purpose. It was because he could. He was free. His expression of freedom was being able to get into his car with his daughter and just drive around and look around and go wherever he wanted to go. He wasn't restricted to a particular part of the city or town or a bunker.

"Sometimes he would talk, but a lot of times he wouldn't. It was very quiet, because I wanted to talk about his past and his history. And he wasn't prepared to discuss any of that. We spent a lot of time just being quiet and being together and looking around. And even today, when I go back to New Jersey and spend time with my dad, sometimes I'll now just drive him around, and we'll just look at places. Sometimes we talk and sometimes we don't.

"A few years back, an old boyfriend of mine took me out riding on the back of his motorcycle. My connection to that sense of riding and to my childhood was immediate…that sense of freedom was so strong. I now own two Harleys and ride exclusively on the back. I cannot even operate them. I love the American brand symbolism, the freedom, and the endless possibility of the open road…all imprinted on me at an early age with my dad on our Sunday afternoon drives.

"That's one of the key things my father taught me—to love your freedom and to love everything that you're entitled to. Everyone hates paying taxes. Not my father. My father knows that if you're paying taxes, you have some freedom. You have the ability to earn money and own things. And he thinks it's a privilege."

In 2008 Jeanne and her sister took their dad back to Germany and Poland. They visited his old apartment, the university in Munich, the cave her father lived in and the cold rocks he slept upon. They visited the one remaining family member, and youngest daughter of the family who had hid him, a woman named Sabina. "It was amazingly wonderful to bring my father to a place where he could reconnect with literally the one surviving person that we know of who knew him during the war and knew he hid in the bunker for so many months. That was powerful.

"She recognized him immediately. He recognized her immediately. They embraced. Sabina was crying. It was like they had never parted. They talked for hours."

I asked Jeanne if her father cried, too. She didn't know. She's only seen her father cry once, she said, when they visited Auschwitz. "It's beyond comprehension how massive Auschwitz and Birkenau are. Brick bunkers and barbed wire as far as the eye can see. It was 90 degrees the day we went there.

"There's a part of the tour where you're at the entrance of Birkenau and you see the railroad tracks that go all the way back, like, two miles or more, to where the crematoria are. And that's where the memorial is. So in this 90 degree heat, my father and I and my sister and some cousins of ours walked the entire length of this track. My 85-year-old dad, we're worried about dehydration, his stamina both physically and emotionally. We haven't eaten. There's no place to sit.

"My sister, who is a doctor, kept saying, 'Dad, you've got to have some water. You're going to pass out in this heat.' My father was like, 'No way, no way.' He would not ever disrespect the souls that walked that track, by having water. His determination was unflappable. He was compelled at 85 years of age in the blazing heat of this camp to pay respects to those who had passed before him at the hands of the Nazis.

"When we finished that walk, we were sitting outside the gates. We were back at Auschwitz and we had just seen the movie they show you. It is a brutal film showing what was found at the camps after liberation. And so my father was telling us that right after the war, he went to Dachau. One of the officials of the town, in approaching this memorial in Dachau, required everyone to take off their shoes, because this ground was holy, because Jews had died in the name of God in this place. And as my father was describing how he took off his shoes and approached this memorial, he broke down and he cried."

Her trip with her father to his birthplace brought Jeanne closer to understanding who she is and why. "I already knew that I never like to waste food, because I know my father was always hungry in those days. I know that I always like to be warm, because my father was always cold. I know that I am very observant of our traditions in the Jewish religion, because those were things that he was denied. So there are certain things that are very obvious to me in my behavior and in my life.

"But Poland really put together a couple of things that weren't as obvious to me, like my father was very tenacious. When I began listening to some of my father's stories about how he survived and the people he knew and the groups in the society that he would interface with somewhat intentionally—like he knew subconsciously that you have to be able to integrate yourself into different parts of the society in order to survive and for me, in order to be accepted and be secure.

"A lot of my interest in these counter-cultural or sub-cultural groups comes indirectly from my dad. He was teaching me very indirectly that you've got to be able to play in a lot of sandboxes in life very nicely and very subtly and you need to have your own agenda, but you need to be part of different mixes of people, to get along and survive.

"I think the other thing that came to the surface is that I have tremendous difficulty putting down roots and staying in one place at one time. I've always preferred multiple places and multiple settings and being with lots of people. In Poland, I kind of put it together that because so much of my father's world was taken away from him, because it was all in one place, I have compensated for that and I choose to live in different worlds and have friends and relationships in different places, as to not lose it all.

"That came to me as I watched my father walk his town and everything was gone and there was nothing there that he could claim he owned or was his. And I think I've carried that burden for many years, in the way I'm going to do these different things to create a mosaic, so that if one goes away, I have another that I can easily continue. That was very profound for me to put that together and understand how my life has emerged, that I'm very comfortable moving about and being unsettled, being a little bit of a wanderer, because you might lose less that way.

"When we went to Poland and I began this level of introspection, I was like, 'Oh, yeah, that's what's going on, fear of loss.' I also have other characteristics, like I have tremendous redundancy in my life. I have two pairs of shoes in Boston; I have the same two pairs of shoes in New Jersey; I have the same two pairs of shoes in Chicago; I have the same two pairs of shoes at my sister's house. So if one goes away, I've got another to fall back on.

"It also affects your relationships. I create some natural barriers, so that if someone is taken away from me, I've already protected myself. I think my father had to create those barriers, too, stemming from the loss of his parents and not being able to trust people for many years. So I think I developed some of that same hard shell around myself.

"Emotionally, my father is very strong. But he has trained himself to suppress a lot of emotion. We didn't grow up in what I'll call an extremely loving environment. There was no animosity. There was no violence, no abuse. There was nothing of that sort. But we did not grow up in an affectionate environment. He was a responsible father. He provided for us. But he was not the kind of dad that you sat down and said, 'Hey, Dad, I got a problem at school. I'm not getting along with so and so. I could really use your advice.' I don't think I had a lot of interaction with my dad in grammar school and high school, and really even in college.

"It wasn't until well after college and I was working. 1995, I think, was probably the beginning of the breakthrough, because 1995 was the reunion of my father's classmates in Israel. There must have been two or three hundred of them who all attended universities in Germany and were survivors. And it was just a big party and an amazing Tower of Babel as everyone spoke so many different languages. That was the beginning, because it was at that meeting that I stepped into this group and became embraced and began to build this foundation of coordinating these survivor reunions. That was the start of my true relationship with my dad."

The story that I wondered about when we started our interview was taking shape: A woman lives in airplanes and hotels because of what she learned early in life about attachment, risk of loss, and intimacy. Jeanne has thrown herself into her career. I asked her if she ever thought she was living in fear of intimacy, because of the risk of not having it returned.

"I absolutely think that," she replied. "It's clearly one of the determining factors why I have stayed single and why I create some amount of emotional distance between the men I do get involved with and is one of the reasons why I probably will not marry. I don't think I would be a good spouse. I don't think I know how.

"I don't really know how to talk about the things that matter. And I also tend to date men that I have a sense are going to be okay not going there. I get my emotional satisfaction and my emotional support with men through my platonic relationships. I've yet to find that one person to really connect with. It would take a lot of work on that person's part to go there with me, because I sense I'm pretty held back by this."

The one man she remains tied with emotionally is her father. And Jeanne knows her time left with him is limited. "One of the things that I haven't reconciled in my mind yet—and I'm not sure you ever deal with this until you have to—is because my father has been such a strong force in my life, I am not sure how I'm going to deal with that when he moves on. One of my real fears is that I'm not going to be able to deal with it and I will have a very strong preference to move on with him." Jeanne began to cry as she explained further, "I'm afraid I won't know how to approach the world or deal with the world when I have to suffer that loss.

"Obviously, with each passing day of each passing year, that ultimate reality does get closer. I've always said, when I've had things that have been really hard to cope with, 'Well, I have to get through this, because my dad is still here.' But I fear that when he's not, I won't know how to cope with that. I'm very afraid of that.

"If there's any one thing that I wish I could redo, I wish I'd pushed those boundaries with my dad a little bit earlier and a little bit more forcefully, because the rewards were wonderful for both me and my dad. I credit my dad with much of my personal and professional success in life. My dad will always be the treasure of my life."

I Don't Feel Like
I Have Anybody

Leilani, who was 39 when we met, was born and raised in Hawaii. She is of Hawaiian, Portuguese, and Scots Irish ancestry. She is a single mother raising two children, who were eight and ten at the time of our interview.

What made Leilani's story compelling was the prominent role played by her stepfather, and how that relationship came to an end. One of his last messages to her was to do everything she could to re-establish a relationship with her biological father.

In our interview, Leilani refers to her biological father as her father, and to her stepfather as her dad.

Leilani's father Leland was born in Seattle in the mid-1940s and grew up there. He was the second of three children growing up in what Leilani calls "a family of intellectuals" that also had an affinity for outdoor living, sports, and music. "Art and history and education were very important in my father's family. There was lots of both national and international travel, and lots of friends from other cultures."

Her parents met in 1962 at Western Washington University. "It was an active, happy relationship with no big hurdles. The stories are all very fond and happy. They moved to Tacoma when they were both graduate students at the University of Puget Sound. My mom had never counted on, and I will say honestly never wanted, kids. She was told she could never have them. So she had planned for a very intellectual life. She was studying to go to law school, and was focused on politics and living an intellectual life with an artistic husband.

"Then she got pregnant and had twins. And that absolutely changed the course of the life she had planned. To try to save the marriage, they decided to move to Hawaii. They thought it would help if they were in Hawaii with my mom's family, with the additional family support that comes with large extended families all participating in raising each other's families."

That attempt didn't work, and Leilani's parents were divorced within a few years.

Leilani has mixed memories of the time together with her father, who had been trained in fine arts through college and graduate school. "My father is very eclectic. Maybe that comes with being an artist and what you have to be able to tap into to create those kinds of things. He was a competitive gymnast and an avid skier. I remember him walking on his hands when I was a little kid and doing all kinds of fun acrobatics. He's also a very accomplished artist, drawing and sculpting, painting and pottery.

"When we were really little, I remember camping and my father telling these stories that he had heard, stories about Coffee Joe the Cowboy and all his adventures. And when we played with Lincoln Logs and Tinker Toys, he was the very engaged parent who would connect with us on that level. When you're really little, that works. But as you start getting older, that doesn't work so well. I was feeling like I needed to parent him.

"We're wired very differently. He lived in an artistic community and for a while, when he had no money, he lived in his studio at the University of Hawaii. And that was very uncomfortable and strange for me. I stopped wanting to spend weekends with him because it was just a really uncomfortable environment."

Several years after Leilani's parents divorced, her father left the Hawaiian Islands and returned to the mainland. Leilani recalls feeling relief when he moved away, "because then I didn't have to be around that. I never felt unsafe or unprotected. I just thought he was weird. And I felt like, 'Who's the grownup?' I felt like I was more responsible than he was, and I often felt in the background of whatever he was working on at the time. I understand that it was a lot about him having to pay the bills and do what needed to be done.

"I also was angry, because what I didn't understand as a child, and do now, was that he really disappeared. I had a lot of resentment, because my opinion is you divorce your spouse, not your child. And he kind of disappeared like he divorced us."

Leilani said she didn't make it easy on him. "I had high expectations and I've never been afraid to verbalize those. I know that he felt really conflicted about living up to what was expected of him and what he was dealing with on his own, the heartbreak of my mom leaving him and not feeling good enough, not living up to her expectation of what life was supposed to look like and be. I didn't know that as a child. I think that disconnect for him was more about emotional survival. He just was raw on the inside and unable to be constantly involved, because it was a reminder of hurt, disappointment, and letdown.

"And yet I still felt really connected to him, because he was so easy to get at; there was no guard with him; you could ask him anything. He was very emotionally available and always has been. My mom said that when we were sick, he was the person we wanted. He was the primary parent. Before they got divorced, when we were hurt or sad or sick, he was the one we went to, which makes a lot of sense, because my mom, to this day, says, 'I don't do babies. I don't like little kids.' And it's true.

"I think that nurturing his artistic spirit through this intellectual life that she envisioned would have been fine, when you didn't add two kids. And as they saw it, one of them could go on with their career and the other one couldn't, and she gave up hers. She really resented it. He was so emotionally raw that when they had these two children, he met us at our level and then, as my mom puts it, she had another kid to raise."

We talked about what Leilani absorbed from her father. "His love of art and music is definitely part of who I am. I've learned to embrace being emotionally available and that it's okay to be transparent sometimes and that you're not weak for being that way."

I wondered if she had found herself in adulthood replicating relationships with men who were somehow broken, less than fully responsible, or free-spirited. She said she had, and a wide smile crossed her face. "I was really afraid of relationships for most of my life. I didn't even date or have my first boyfriend until college. I had disastrous relationships from the very beginning, which is probably why, in the four years I've been separated and divorced, I've dated very little."

Leilani moved to the mainland to attend college, and soon found herself in an abusive relationship with one of the football team's star players. "I did his homework. He never had time to study. I was easily convinced that the physical abuse was my fault. On the outward side of life, he was the most fun guy on the football team, everybody's best friend. So because everybody else loved him so much, I thought well, it must be me.

"That paralleled how it was growing up for me, because all my friends thought my mom was just the greatest and that we had such a great everything. And all the while, I really despised my mom. The pressures were just too much. When I failed, it was always because I hadn't tried hard enough.

"So I was trying to rescue that abusive relationship in the same way I tried to survive growing up at home. And then the next serious relationship was with another guy on the football team who had already graduated and was in medical school. We had a really good relationship. I moved to Seattle and we dated long distance for three years. And then he broke up with me and absolutely broke my heart. I was super connected with his whole family. It was a very wholesome, traditional family. And that's the life that I wanted, a normal, traditional family life.

"And so it was very devastating when that didn't work out, but it was good that it didn't work out, too. Because I didn't then and I still don't really trust the whole idea of marriage. I've never really seen it work. And while I really wanted kids, I never wanted to actually get married."

Leilani got that wish, sort of. Within eight months of that crushing breakup, she met her husband-to-be. "It was a whirlwind. He moved in with me and three months later, we were engaged and a year later, we were married. I remember feeling really numb. I loved the dating part of it, because he was a real doting dater, very romantic. And he was great as a new husband. But after we had kids, he started the disconnect and later said, 'Well, that's what you do when you're dating. You don't do that when you're married.'"

I wanted to explore Leilani's deep belief that marriage can't be trusted. So we talked about that, and whether it came from her childhood experience.

"Probably, yeah. Even though my mom remarried, they had a horrible relationship. She was a yeller and a tyrant and nothing was ever good enough. She treated him the same way she treated us kids. And so to me, marriage doesn't look right. Even though she got remarried, that still wasn't normal.

"I only know of two or three marriages that have lasted that were good. How scary is that? Every one of my friends has divorced parents. I know it can exist, but to me, it's the exception, not the rule. So I still don't believe it will happen for me. That's kind of sad, and because the one chance I took didn't work out, it's like I proved my theory.

"So would I like another relationship in life? Yeah. But I don't have a lot of hope or expectation that that will happen. I believe in monogamy. I believe in committed relationships. I have a very strong Christian faith. I just don't know that in our day and age, it can actually exist.

"I'm still searching for that happy medium between my father and his emotional availability and my dad, who was really protective and more of that traditional guy's guy. He fished. He could fix things. He was ex-military. So I've always been searching for this impossible equation of an emotionally available guy's guy."

Leilani's dad—her stepfather—came into her life early. He and Leilani's mother had known each other since childhood. Shortly after the divorce, they came together and were married. He had children from his first marriage, and the families melded easily. "I was in fourth grade when they married. He never treated us any differently than he treated his own kids, from the very beginning. I was the only girl and so I got a lot of extra attention. I think he was happy to have a daughter around."

One of her earliest memories is of her dad laying down the law.

"I remember my mom saying I couldn't have this pair of shorts and so I asked him for them and he got them for me. And then, it was a big blowup about it and he came to me and he didn't get super pissed. He was just like, 'You can't do that again. It was not fair, because she had said no. I am here for you, but you cannot set us up like that again. I'm not going to allow it.' That was the end of it. He set the ground rules really clearly. And I never crossed them again. It made me feel like I could talk to him about anything, anything at all.

"There wasn't one thing I couldn't tell him or didn't tell him. I told him, not my mom, when I got pregnant on accident when I was just out of college and I didn't know what to do. I felt like I had a place."

I told Leilani I found it interesting that her feelings of attachment to her dad strengthened after she was disciplined. She began to cry.

"He died about ten years ago. It's hard to talk about him, because he's gone and he was the one person I really connected with as my parent. When things went wrong, he was the one person I could go to. And I don't feel like I have anybody. So it's hard that he's gone."

Leilani continued crying as she spoke of her dad being the one to walk down the aisle with her when she got married. He was already ill, and had only a few years left to live. It wasn't perfect, but it was real and it was true and it was trusted and it was safe and it was all of those things that you want in a parent, especially as a daughter.

"He did all the guy stuff. And he played sports and he kept the yard. And he worked really hard. He always wanted my mom to have the best of everything, and just doted on me and adored me as the girl and was the flip side with my brothers, kind of hard on them, but so proud. When he talked about us, he'd gleam with pride and he was always so encouraging and just a *dad*. He taught the hard lessons that needed to be taught, but was also the soft place to land when I needed the soft place to land, the protector."

Against the backdrop of his crumbling marriage to her mother, Leilani's dad stepped up as a father and parented her with love and determination. His was a hero's journey, I thought. I told her that.

"Totally," she said. "I never felt like I was anything but just the same as if I had been his biological kid. He absolutely adored my mom and through thick and thin, good and bad, continued to the end of his life to try to make her happy, and live up to her expectations of him. He never stopped trying, ever.

"He was a really fun guy. He had this sort of grumpy old man personality to him in a lot of ways, and was just sort of gruff. But he had this real soft side to him when it came to me. And he was really hard-working but didn't always succeed.

"He owned his own insurance agency and my whole life, that's what he did. He ended up with a gambling problem and he lost his business to it. But I think it was the constant pressure to live up to my mom's expectations of what providing looked like. I think it got to feel impossible. It got to feel impossible to me just as a kid, to live up to her expectations.

"So I can see how the pressures of that could breed reaching out to things like that. Obviously, he made that choice and there was some addictive part of his personality that took hold. Maybe I blame my mom for too much, but I think the catalyst for that was trying to live up to her expectations. Outside of that, he was just a good-natured, really involved parent and always available, always there. He participated in our sports, was there for every swim meet. And when my mom wouldn't come to my track meets, she couldn't be bothered, my dad came to every single one of them."

In the years that followed, Leilani watched her dad's health, finances, and marriage deteriorate. "I know that it was the beginning of a lot of really bad years for my dad, searching and trying to duplicate that success and be good enough for my mom. It was a lot of stress and pressure on him. My mom actually kicked him out. She divorced him, because she didn't want to be financially responsible for him, though they only lived apart for about eight months. Then they lived back together again and he always wanted to get remarried, but she never would.

"He went door-to-door selling mouthwash and pantyhose that don't run and tried selling cell phone card plans before those were really a thing and doing multi-level marketing and tried any number of things to make something go. And he never could make it go. I think that stress was the catalyst for him getting sick. That loss was humiliating and I don't think he ever recovered from it.

"I felt more like it was my turn to take care of him. I ended up putting a credit card in both of our names to try to help, and tried to be there for him in all those ways he was there for me. He never used the credit card. But I just couldn't imagine him not having a safety net, because my mom had cut him off. She wouldn't help him and she was like, 'Tough luck, it's your fault.'

"I thought this could happen to me, too, because I know how desperate that need to live up to that expectation is and you'll just do whatever you need to do. I connected with him and I understood how he could have made the bad choices he did, because of feeling so inadequate, because I felt that same way with my mom my whole life.

"But he let me be who I was, and that was real tenderhearted. He never put me down or made me feel like I couldn't cry if I needed to cry, feel bad if I needed to feel bad, feel disappointed if I needed to feel disappointed. He didn't sit there and have long, emotional conversations with me."

Leilani broke down and sobbed again as she thought back to the last time she saw the man who was there for her as a child, at her wedding, and who refused to shrink as her father, even if he was selling mouthwash and pantyhose door-to-door.

"I took my son home when he was three months old to see my dad. And he was 80 pounds, but getting up and walking every day, accomplishing something every day. When it was time for me to go, and my mom was taking us to the airport, he was standing at the front door waving and smiling. And I got out of the car five or six times, got back in and out of the car, because I knew when I left I would never see him again.

"And the last time, he said, 'Baby, you have to go. You're going to miss your plane.' And I said, 'But if I go, then this is the last time I'm going to hug you, the last time I'm going to hold you.' And I knew it and he knew it. And I'm just crying and he started to cry. And he said, 'It's not the last time. We'll see each other again.' He was a very spiritual person, and that's what he was referring to. And he had tears running down his face.

"I think it's remarkable that he was able to be the kind of father he was, because his dad was an absolute jerk. He was mean, he was verbally awful and was ridiculously hard on my dad. They grew up pretty poor, and my dad was the provider and caretaker for his siblings. And I think my dad worked really hard to be everything that my Grandpa wasn't, and to be available and to not be a mean bastard.

"I had a very remarkable dad. Right before he died he asked me to give my father another chance. He said, 'I know this is hard for you, but just think about it in terms of you don't need a father. Just get to know him as a man and a person and let him be a grandfather.' There was no insecurity about that at all. So I think it came from a place of real enlightenment, but also wisdom and absolute security and unselfishness.

"My dad knew my kids would need a grandpa and he saw my father's positives. I think he also saw where my father and I have a lot of similarities and knew that the emotional connection that I didn't have with my mom could be found in my father. And because my dad asked, I've given my father another chance, and I have a pretty remarkable relationship with him that is growing in emotional connection and understanding and depth.

"I thought to myself that maybe in doing that, it can resolve some of the things as a child I didn't have, but that he's now able to give to my kids. So I've gotten to know him as a man and a person and I've started to really love him and adore and appreciate who he is and how many similarities we really do have.

"He's also very sick now and so there are a lot of parallels for me with my relationship with my dad that are hard. He has adult onset primary progressive MS and Parkinson's on top of it. And his health is failing pretty quickly and he's only 66. It's hard to watch another father die."

Run for Your Life

Losing a parent is never easy. Losing a father when you're a little girl is devastating.

Kara Goucher is a professional distance runner and was a member of the US Olympic team in 2008. Her father was killed in a car accident by a drunk driver shortly before she turned four. Kara was 31 when we met.

Kara's biological father, Mirko, was born in 1948 in Zablace, Croatia, which at the time was Yugoslavia. Four of his siblings died during childbirth. Another died from food poisoning when she was three or four years old. Mirko grew up as the youngest of three children. His family lived on the Adriatic Sea in a small town where, as Kara described it, "everybody knows everybody, everyone's related, and very poor.

"When my dad was four years old, my grandfather went to war. He was stationed in the States for some reason, and basically fled and stayed in New York City. He earned enough money to bring over one person and he brought over my uncle. They started an insulation business, and they earned enough money to finally bring my grandma, my aunt, and my dad over. Meanwhile, nine years had gone by. So my dad didn't see his dad for nine years."

Her father earned a soccer scholarship to Ottawa University in Kansas where he met his wife-to-be. He prepared himself in school for a role in his family's business and got married. Kara was the second of the couple's three daughters.

The drunk driver who cut her father's life short also did the same to Kara's memories. "I don't really have many. I have two or three, but I don't know if it's just stories I've heard so many times, or actual memories. This isn't really a memory, it's something my mom's told me. My father had fallen out of the back of his Jeep and broke both of his wrists. Both of his arms were in casts and the movie "Bambi" had come out and he was going to take my sister and me to see it. And I was just being so bad and he was like, 'You're going to get a spanking,' and I was like, 'You can't. Your arms are broken.'

"My dad still played soccer for fun. He started a Croatian league in the area and coached in a girls' league. I feel like I remember him coming home from a game with cuts and bruises and him having me kiss them to make them feel better."

I asked Kara how that memory feels. "It makes me feel happy. I used to feel like he didn't know me or I don't know him. But when my sister-in-law had a daughter and I got to watch her grow up and see before she turned four how influenced she was, and how aware she was of my brother-in-law and how really into her he was, that was very healing for me. I wish I could pull out memory after memory after memory. But I feel like there was this connection and there was love.

"When I ran the New York City marathon a couple of years ago, my mom gathered all these pictures, because the course runs within two blocks of where he was killed. My mom had all these pictures of me flexing my muscles for him, and playing soccer with him. It was really a heavy race. It's just so much bigger of a deal than the Olympics or anything for my family that I was running there. And that was just two years ago, but it was very healing, even all this time later, to see the pictures.

"When I was in college, I was kind of in the stage of, 'I don't know who I am.' That's when I went to Croatia and saw where he grew up. Because after my mom got remarried, we didn't talk about my dad for about ten years. I was twenty when my mom got divorced, and all that came crashing down. She found a tape with his voice on it and all sorts of stuff. So, I feel like there's this period in my life where I never even talked about him. There's this ten, twelve-year block where there were no pictures up, whereas now, it's much more open. I've established a much closer relationship with my aunt and I can talk with her about stuff. I feel like I have a much better grasp on all of that now than I did back then.

"My stepfather's first wife was horribly murdered. And she and my dad just weren't talked about. He had three kids and my mom had three kids and it was like, 'We're going to make this blended family and everyone's going to get along great.' And they meant well, I believe. I think they just were like, 'This is the easiest way. The kids are all still young. Everyone will just mesh and it'll be this big, happy thing.' But I think in their effort to try to make it easier on everyone, we all ended up with a lot of hurt and wounds from it, because we all just felt like we had to deny this whole part of us."

I couldn't imagine having that part of one's experience cleaned from the slate and not have access to it emotionally. We talked about what that was like.

"As a child that loses a parent, you just want to know. I used to tell my mom, 'I don't even know what he sounds like.' Or I can't just ask him something stupid, like, 'What's your favorite color; what did you think when you first saw my mom; why did you want to name me Kara?' You know, just stupid things that really don't matter, but you could ask someone so easily.

"I did have a stepfather during that period, so I tried to pour all of that onto him to a certain extent. All of my wanting to know who I am. I wanted more from him than he could give me. And that ended up hurting me later in life, because this relationship that I had built up so much didn't exist. I am not angry at my mother at all. I don't resent what she did one bit. I feel like she was just trying to survive.

"But for me and my two biological sisters, it was painful, especially as we became adults and started our own families, just to have closed that off for so long. Hindsight's always twenty-twenty, and my mom regrets the way things were handled. But I was afraid to even ask things. I didn't even know when my dad died when I was growing up. I couldn't tell you the date and I was afraid to bring it up. I would have felt like I was doing something wrong.

After Kara's father was killed, her mother moved the family from New York to Minnesota so she could raise her daughters near her own family. As a result, Kara saw little of her father's family for years.

"My aunt or my grandparents would come to visit and they were strangers to me. I didn't even try to engage with them, because what was I going to talk to them about? Everything I wanted to know, I couldn't ask them. I had one picture. I don't know how I got it and it was, like, hidden in my dresser. It was a picture of my mom and my dad. It was Easter Sunday, and my mom is holding me, and my dad's holding my sister, and I have no idea how I got my hands on that picture.

"My little sister and I will say that we can be really cold and people can read us the wrong way. But, really, we're the most sensitive people on the planet. We just feel everything. And for me, it's made me be really open. I will tell anybody anything, because I don't ever want to feel that way again, like something's off limits or that something's wrong because I want to know something. It's just made me way more honest. I'll just tell people things. My husband will be like, 'I can't believe you talked about that.' But I just don't care. My life is basically an open book.

"My uncle died four years ago and my grandparents three or four years ago and I feel like I lost an opportunity to know who I am more. And that's painful to me. I'm not mad. I'm just sad that they were coming into my home twice a year and I never asked them anything. It was always awkward. There was an opportunity there and I lost it. My aunt is great; she will tell me anything. And she's done such a good job of helping both my sisters and I heal from all of it. But I still wish I could go back and not be afraid to ask."

Kara talked freely about the feelings that she carried into adulthood from losing her father and not being able to openly explore that with her family.

"When I got married, I remember saying, 'I have had a hole in myself for just wondering and not being able to find peace for so long and I finally have peace.' And I do feel like Adam has done that for me. But if I really dig down, I still feel I'm missing something, a little bit at the core. It's just not there. That hole gets closed up a little bit more each year. The more I learn, and especially running that marathon in New York—it's so silly, it's just a race—but it was so therapeutic for my whole family. Everyone was there where this horrible tragedy happened and yet they were celebrating."

I was struck by her commenting that she still feels like she's missing something. I don't think a void that big ever goes away. I think the best we can do is make peace with it. And so I shared that thought with her. She agreed. "Right. It gets better. When I look back at my childhood, I wasn't like, 'I don't know who my dad is; I'm so sad.' I felt nothing. There was no sadness. There was no feeling like I was being cheated. It was just such a part of my life. My mom says, 'I remember you coming home and saying, 'We did this project at school and I just want to have a dad.' But I don't remember feeling that way."

Part of what helped Kara's healing was visiting her father's grave site. As a girl she would ride her bicycle there with her sisters, and they would pull weeds from the site, clean it up, and decorate it. "We would leave all sorts of stuff—pinecones, notes, little plastic flowers, little bows, just random stuff. It wasn't an emotional thing, really, when I was little. I would never cry or anything, not until I was older. If I went there now, I would start crying, but never then. When I was older, I went over there a lot more with my high school friends. I left pictures, like my graduation pictures."

I asked if we could talk about the notes she left, and what feelings she remembered in leaving those notes and flowers. The notes, she said, were about, "This is what I'm doing. My dance recital's coming up. Love you.' When I started running, I'd go tell him about that. 'Mom says I get it from you.' It's kind of sad when I say it out loud, but it didn't seem sad. It was just like a diary entry, kind of.

"I always wanted approval or love or just to have him know me. That can make me start crying right now." And then she did begin to cry. "It's like, 'This is my way. This is who I am. Please pay attention.' I used to pray to God that he would please just know who I am, that he would be able to pick me out if he saw me, all these years later, that he would be able to say, 'That's my daughter.'"

When Kara's mother remarried, Kara gained a new father-daughter relationship. And just like a marriage, a stepfather-stepdaughter relationship unfolds for better, for worse. "For the first five years of that marriage, I threw everything into it. Like, this is my dad, I love him so much. And it wasn't until later that I started to see, 'This isn't what I want it to be.'

"Overall, my childhood was happy. When my mom remarried, there were six of us kids; there was always someone to play with; everyone was involved in a lot of stuff; I was exposed to so many things. We lived in a beautiful house by a park. We were always outside making sled trails. I have so many great memories. So when I look back, everything's happy until about high school. And then I had running and my friends.

"Unless I really pick it apart, I don't look back at it and feel like it was a bad childhood. My mom is like, 'I'm so sorry.' But I'm a totally normal person, you know? And I don't remember it being horrible, unless I really break it down. And then I think, 'Well, that was actually quite unhealthy for a while.'

"When I think back, I don't think negative things. I think of the good stuff. My dad coached my softball team. He coached one of my soccer teams. He was very involved in anything to do with athletics. I think of all six of us getting in the car and driving from Duluth, Minnesota to Disneyland, with our little turtle on the top and we each had our own color of a hockey bag filled with our clothes. But as far as, like, 'I'm struggling with this; I don't know what to do about this; I'm not sure how I feel about this,' he wasn't available.

"I am thankful for everything he did for me when I was growing up. He really supported me in all of my athletic endeavors and he came to all my school functions. He had six kids, you know, and he really did support us, financially allowed me to do all those things. And I am so thankful. My life is peaceful now. And when I visit my family, it's peaceful."

Part of filling her loss was Kara's finding surrogate fathers in her coaches. "I have really close relationships with my coaches, which are always men. It doesn't take a rocket scientist to figure out I'm always looking for that sort of relationship, that approval and that connection that I don't have in another place in my life.

"I was so attached to my high school coach. I was so attached to my college coach. And when I had to leave my college coach, it was—I could start crying, just remembering what it was like to have to leave him. And with my coach now, I love him to pieces. And I definitely overdo that, looking for that. My coach now, I've told him, 'I don't want to think of you as a father. I love you so much, and you've influenced my life so much, but I never want to put that on you.' So, yeah, my coaches have all been really influential and they've all been men."

The last area we explored was Kara's relationships with men, and how her beliefs about men, love, and intimacy were shaped by the loss of her first loving relationship with a man, her father.

"Well, I think it caused me to have some dysfunction with some relationships. You know, like my college coach. I definitely put too much on him and he took it on, too. Then it was like he shouldn't have known necessarily all these details of my life and I shouldn't have been going to him for everything. He's a college coach and he has a million things going on.

"I trust men that are in a position of authority, maybe more than I should sometimes. And that trust has been betrayed, but nothing like super bad. And I'm shocked by it, you know. Maybe I shouldn't have been quite so trusting. I knew this person on a certain level, but maybe I shouldn't have thought it was so much deeper than that.

"It's always been with people that are older and in a position of authority over me. It's never someone my age. I don't have inappropriate relationships or anything like that. I just have made them into more than they should be. But now I just see how silly it can be. I'm like, 'Why didn't I just see that? Why did I have to try to create this relationship with other people?' Not everybody has that fairy tale relationship.

"Most of my friends are very close with their fathers and I'm envious, you know? I'm envious that when Father's Day comes around, my best friend can go and buy a card off the shelf that's mushy and everything in that prewritten card rings true. And I don't have that. But I'm tired of feeling sorry for myself about it. For so long, I just felt sorry for myself. This is crazy. My life is so fulfilling. Get over it, you know what I mean? The relationships that I have are wonderful."

When Kara and I met for coffee a week before our interview, I found out she was more than four months pregnant. When we met for our interview a few weeks later, she'd found out she and her husband Adam, also a world-class runner, were having a boy.

"I was scared at first when I found out it was a boy, because I just know women so much better. But now I feel like it's supposed to be. This is, for me, another chapter on getting to know my dad. So I'm excited about it. I'm not going to put pressure on this kid to be anything that he's not, but I feel like it's going to give me a window."

A few weeks after our interview, I asked Kara if she and her husband could come over to our house and autograph pictures for my daughters. They did. Six months later, I heard from Kara by email. Her son was nine weeks old and healthy.

A little more than three months after her son's birth, Kara was competing again at an elite level. She and Adam named their son Colton Mirko Goucher. He goes by the name "Colt." It's a fitting name for the son of two world-class runners. And his middle name, Mirko, is in honor of Kara's father.

He Has to Love Me

Hana was among those women who had reservations about doing an interview with me. I used to see her at the gym near my office, though we'd never met. I wasn't sure if she was from the Middle East or Northern Africa, but I was still looking for women from both areas. So one day I walked up and introduced myself.

We chatted for about five minutes. She was a quiet woman, with a soft presence and beautiful accent. She was 39 and at the time divorced, with no children. Hana didn't seem uncomfortable with my request, but said she'd think about it and let me know. So I gave her my card and assumed I'd hear back if she was interested. Perhaps a month after we'd met, Hana said she was ready to share her story. After she'd shared it with me, I understood her reluctance.

Hana's father was born in Somalia in 1939 in a small town called Jig Jigga, close to the Ethiopian border. The odds weren't in his favor from the beginning. His mother's previous four children had died at birth. When Hana's father was born, his mother had already prepared a burial for him.

While he and two younger sisters survived, he had a father only until he was six years old. Hana's grandmother raised all three children herself. "They grew up very poor," Hana told me, "as my grandmother was single and uneducated. Back then, woman didn't have a chance to go to school. I think she sold food to survive."

Hana's father came to the US to study agriculture, and after two years went back to Somalia. Hana, her older brother, and closest sister were born and raised in a small coastal town called Kisimayo outside of Mogadishu. They later moved to Saudi Arabia.

Hana recalls her father being "very hard, very strict. We didn't really do things like a father and daughter. He was committed to work, and we stayed at home with my mom. There is one picture at the house when I was nine, ten months, with my dad holding me in his lap and my oldest brother standing there. That's the only picture I remember of me sitting in my father's lap. I don't remember ever jumping to Dad, as 'Oh, Dad, how are you? I miss you.' I have no memory of that.

"Part of the culture is you don't really show you're emotional. We don't say, 'I love you.' I never said to my father, 'I love you.' But I am his daughter and he knows I will always love him. Whatever come, I will always be there for him.

"We were always afraid of him, because he will get upset if we do anything wrong. Saudi Arabia is a very strict culture, especially for a woman. We used to take care of my little brothers. We have to feed them and when they finish eating, we have to make sure that they took a nap. So, if they didn't have a nap, my dad used to yell at us. We didn't have a childhood where I could ride a bike or play with the girls outside. We grew up like adult. I liked my father, but we didn't feel like he was emotionally caring about us. He was very strict. He was very disciplined.

"My oldest brother had a lot of issues with my dad and he would never forgive him. When he was younger, my dad was emotionally abusive to him. 'You have to do an excellent job in your school because I'm paying money to bring you to the States and it's international money. It cost me thousands. So, you have to be this and this.' It's like nothing is good enough. He never told us, 'Oh, you guys did a good job. I'm really happy for you. And I'm so proud of you.'

"As we got older and confronted him, we said, 'Dad, you were rough and tough.' And he said, 'All this is for you guys. I want the best for you. And if I didn't want you to go out with your girlfriends, if I didn't want you to get drunk and do all this bad stuff, that was a good thing for you.'

"I think part of it is because my dad grew up with a single mother. He didn't really see a loving father. And my grandmother was very, very strict. And I think he carried the same thing to us. He didn't know how to show love and caring. Dad would put everybody down.

"I remember when I was young, around twelve, we'd be all sitting in the living room with my mom and when Dad would come home, we'd all run upstairs because he'd carry home all the stress from work. There was no running to your father or hugging. We were all scared of him. He'd be grumpy and complaining that the house was not clean enough. And emotionally he was hard on us, nothing we ever did was good enough.

"I think he did the best he could, but he didn't know how to show love and emotion and care. And that really bothered me. To think about it now, it always bothered me. My dad always criticized us in front of my cousins or his sister, in front of everybody. 'You don't know anything. You be quiet.' It was very painful. I felt disappointed, like nothing is enough, what I do for my father.

"As a child, what you really remember and care about is how loving and caring your dad was, how he was close to you, how you were close to him. You don't really care about what big car Dad buys you or if he pays your tuition. And we didn't get those things. I didn't get those things.

"But, as we grew up, we all confront him and now he's changed. My dad was less restrictive with my younger sister and my youngest brother than when he was with me and my oldest brother."

Hana revisited these childhood relationship issues in the first husband she married. "He was 20-some years older than me and could never show his feeling and his loving, like most Somalian men. And I wanted a man who was caring and loving and could cry and could show his feelings. He wasn't like that. And he reminded me of my dad."

When Hana and I talked about what she took of importance from her father, it was clear that they were lessons that had their roots in some pain. "The important thing, if I would have had kids, is to show my loving and caring to my children. So I learned to really show loving and caring. And the most important thing really for me, I don't criticize people. Because I learned that's the wrong way to do it, and I see it really affected my older brother emotionally.

"I see in the United States sometimes the kids don't talk to their parents, they have no communication, nothing, and you see this old lady by herself and the daughter doesn't phone her or anything. I will never do that to my mother or my dad. They're the ones who brought me into this world and I owe them. Especially my dad, whatever he did, we let it go and we help him. I don't remember one time my dad told me, 'Hana, I love you.' But he's my father. He has to love me. And I'm his daughter and of course I love him."

Not long after our interview, Hana re-married. Having left my job, I stopped going to the gym where I met her. But I contacted her by email about a year after our interview, and she told me she was expecting her first child soon. A few months later, I invited her family over for dinner. She found what she was looking for in her second husband, who is a warm and sensitive man from Pakistan. And as I watched her with her infant, Hana was true to her promise, full of love and compassion for her daughter.

Hana's words continued to ring in my ears following our conversation. *When Dad would come home, we'd all run upstairs because he'd carry home all the stress from work. He'd be grumpy and complaining that the house was not clean enough.*

I couldn't help but think of my own daughters, and the frazzled father who came home to them. I am Hana's father, I realized. And he is me. We're black, we're white. We're yellow and brown. We're rich, we're poor, we're someplace in between. We're the stressed-out fathers from around the world who can't see our way out of the conditions that squeeze our heads like a vise, and that tie our stomachs in knots.

I know something about her father's feelings, the bitterness, the anger, the frustration of feeling trapped. What else do I have in common with him? Are my daughters growing up feeling like nothing is good enough? Do they feel loved? Do they feel safe when I'm around, or on edge?

When my work takes me out of town, the reports I hear when I call home at night are of a pretty calm and happy place. In fact, it sounds more peaceful than when I am there. I can't help but worry as I think about Hana's harsh father. *Is this who I am?*

Holy War

I was intrigued with the idea of letting a therapist tell me her inner story. I had several psychologists offer to do interviews with me. I chose to meet with Noreen, a clinical psychotherapist, wife, and mother who was 55 years old when we met. She came to her profession after confronting her emotional entanglements with her father.

Born in upstate New York in 1926, Noreen's father Paul was the third of five children. His father, of Canadian-English descent, was American-born and Protestant. His mother was Irish Catholic, also American-born. Paul grew up working on a dairy farm and attending a one-room schoolhouse. Later, his parents began growing sweet corn and apples, and they planted apple trees so that their children could go to college from the income those fruit trees produced.

Paul's life—and then Noreen's—was shaped by religious conflict, as his father was staunchly anti-Catholic. "Sundays were extremely tense in his family, in that his mother and the children would always go to church and his father would be somewhat upset about that," she told me. "So that was always part of the mood in the household that was difficult for him."

Hard work, especially on the farm, was one of the principal values that shaped her father, Noreen said. So was education. "His parents were progressive in terms of education. The older sisters are quite academic. One earned a PhD. His oldest sister is kind of an historian. His closest brother became headmaster of a private school and his youngest brother is a physician."

Athletics were highly valued in his family as well, and Paul excelled at football, basketball, and baseball. He studied physical education in college, and later completed a master's degree in public administration. "In 1943, he got drafted," Noreen said. "He took an IQ test when he was drafted and he scored, as he recently informed me, 158. One hundred sixty is genius level, so they sent him to an immersion Japanese school. Then he was sent to Japan to work as an interpreter during the war. He returned to college on the GI Bill and finished."

Paul and his wife met in their early twenties and married a few years later, in 1950. "There's a little religious repetition issue, because my father had this tension around religion growing up; he's a very staunch Catholic, and my mother is Jewish. But she was raised as a secular Jew, and was not particularly religious. It was a problem between my parents, because my mother believed in birth control and my father didn't. So she decided to begin catechism classes and began to study the Catholic religion. And because she knew about the tension in my father's family, she didn't want to have every Sunday be horrible. She converted to Catholicism before she married my father."

The couple had six children. Noreen—born in 1953—was second. Until she was ten, she recalls, her father taught PE in a small-town high school, and coached football, basketball, and baseball. "He loved that. That was really his identity. He also played semi-pro baseball for a while. He was really into sports and my mother was a really good athlete, too. There's a major theme of hard work and a major theme of attention to sports, but for the boys, not the girls. This was all pre-Title IX and there wasn't the kind of attention to girls' athletics that there is now."

Noreen characterized her father as typical of the times. "He would go to work, come home, read the paper while my mother cooked the meals, he would read us stories, tell us stories at bedtime. Up until I was ten, we lived half an hour away from his parents. Every Sunday after church we would go to the farm and sell apples and cider at a farm stand they had. If we stopped at the grocery store I would walk in and see our sweet corn or our apples and I thought I was famous.

"But he was a PE teacher for thirteen years, and then he had six kids. He was making $7,000 a year and he realized he couldn't support his family. And so he got an offer to be assistant to the head of this insurance company that students pay to be insured as athletes. So he essentially would go around to schools in the state or review claims of athletes that had gotten hurt and decide whether they would pay or not. And he hated that job. He missed coaching, he wanted to teach, but he felt he had to do that to support his family. And we moved so we were no longer half an hour to the farm, we were like three and a half hours from the farm.

"He became very depressed. He had a lot of headaches, would put his head down on the dinner table, he would go to his room a lot, he was just less engaged. I was very aware of that as a teenager and how hard it was for my mother.

"We moved to the suburbs. Bigger school, better for me academically, I was immediately pushed into a college track. My brothers did well athletically. And that was a big focus. So at our family dinner table we talked about sports, not schoolwork. I was on the tennis team, and I played field hockey, my sister played field hockey and she was an outstanding swimmer, but that was not part of the conversation. My parents didn't attend our matches or games."

I asked Noreen if she had wanted her father at her athletic events with her, and if she missed his presence. She did. "At the time, Chris Evert was just rising as a star in pro tennis and I remember reading about her. She's my age, and reading how women who have excelled in tennis had very strong fathers and their presence was very important—I remember thinking, 'How come I don't have that?' Not that

I was Chris Evert, but the reason she did so well was because she had this strong presence of her father.

"When I first went into therapy, when I was in grad school, I remember in one of my beginning sessions describing my story, and my therapist said, 'Oh, you were an athlete.' And I was like, 'Yeah!' And I had never considered myself an athlete, even though I played competitive tennis in college. So it was never until much later in my life I came to this sort of revelation that, 'Oh, yeah, I am an athlete.' In my family I wasn't. And that's when I became angry about what wasn't there.

"So that was one major theme, this whole sports thing. The other theme was the whole religion thing, and that was painful. We grew up Catholic. We went to church every Sunday, no meat on Friday, giving stuff up for Lent, fish sticks. All that stuff. We were all baptized, confirmed.

"So that was pretty non-conflictual until as a teenager I started not wanting to go to church, but that wasn't an option. When I went to college I decided I would stop going. I graduated from college and went to Italy, living and working there for about two and a half years. My father would write me these letters: 'What is it like to go to Mass in the language?' So I finally decided to tell him that I didn't go to church and that I hadn't for years. I wrote both my parents, and that just caused a huge rift in our relationship for years.

"My father wrote back and said that could not be. No daughter of his could not be Catholic. He would pray for me but I really couldn't be his daughter. And that was horrific. Here I was across the ocean and he disowned me. I was 23 years old. That was awful. My mother signed the letter, and that killed me. Because I knew my mother had ambivalence about the Catholic Church. And this whole thing that he would pray for me, I was going to go to hell, it was just horrific.

"Then I went to graduate school and did a masters degree in counseling. That was when I first went into therapy. Every time I would go home my father would get sick. Now I understand it, as a psychologist, but my mother would have to take care of him. And I felt guilty, every time I came my father would get sick. It was just awful.

"So that's really when I first went into therapy around those issues, and some boyfriend issues, too. That took years to dissipate and my father could never talk about it directly. Little by little I guess he got over it, but he couldn't say, 'I'm furious with you, you're a heathen.' Instead he would say, 'I don't feel well.' And that was true over the years and is still true. He can't say, 'I'm depressed, or sad, or angry.' He says, 'I don't feel well.'

"My parents got along. Again, my father not being able to express his emotions, they never fought. If they had a disagreement, my father would leave the room. I never can remember my parents arguing. My father couldn't bear it. You couldn't fight with him. He can't bear conflict. I had to learn to fight much later in life. I didn't understand how to bear conflict or even talk about conflictual issues.

"I learned over the years to fight, but I think that was very hard for me in relationships, because I didn't know how to. And my first pretty serious boyfriend in high school was a boy who was depressed. I knew how to do depression. I was an expert at it. So that played itself out in relationships until I had some good therapy. It was in some ways the status quo in terms of men."

Noreen spent the first decade of her early adulthood working out the issues surrounding her relationship with her father. "There were two stages: My very first therapist was a woman. I had a boyfriend in Italy, and he got a fellowship at Columbia. But I wanted to break up with him. And he didn't want to break up. And he became very depressed and had suicidal ideation and that really scared me.

"That was maybe a year of therapy, to help me separate from him and realize that's not my problem, that's him and this is me. Then I went to work, and was dating another man for a number of years who was from South America. He was a psychologist, already established, and he was a very charismatic man and very smart and very interesting. But he cheated on me and I kind of knew it and I had a hard time breaking up with him. I wanted to break up with him and I couldn't.

"That's when I went into therapy the second time. And that's when I really worked out the issues with my father. That was five years of intensive psychotherapy twice a week. It was really about my father even though it started with the boyfriend. Oh my God, I was an athlete, my father was depressed, all this stuff that was floating around in my life, and I was acting it out in ways I didn't know. And I was able to understand my father, forgive him, talk to my mother more. It was right at the end of that therapy that I met Daniel. And he's a pretty healthy guy. We've been married twenty years.

"I finished that therapy in my thirties. It was a long road that has some big father themes for me. So it shaped my life. I remember going to my father's retirement dinner. He was 57 and he'd worked for this company that he hated and someone gave a speech about him. And there were five words they used to describe him, and one was frugal and one was fair. I remember thinking, 'Those aren't really accolades. To be frugal? Fair? Wow, people don't really admire him. There's not like a connection emotionally.'

"It was kind of sad to me. Here's a man, near genius intelligence, he's had a hard time. He's struggled in his life. He's not particularly depressed now. And I would say we have a pretty good relationship, given the parameters. He talks to me, he emails me, sometimes he's a little overly religious, but I just kind of ignore it. We were there this past weekend and my brothers were around and pretty much the conversation was about sports. Still! It's about March Madness, or Michelle who just had a soccer thing happen—he has a pretty narrow range. Although he reads a ton and he's very smart, he's very constricted emotionally.

"My relationship with each of my parents has had a profound impact on my livelihood, where I've lived in the world, and what languages I speak, but also my emotional life, and having been stunted along the way. And I think had I not gone into therapy I wouldn't have become a psychologist. I think it's helped me understand how powerful our early life is. I really could have gotten stuck, and I have gotten stuck along the way with men. I think that's where it can play itself out."

During my conversation with Noreen, I thought a lot about my own daughters. We're not conflicted about religion per se, but I spent eight years before I started this book in a life something like her father's. My religion was professional accomplishment. That was my false god.

Beyond what my daughters had learned from watching me slog through my career missteps, I also hope my safe landing from the corporate mother ship will teach them something. I hope they grow into adulthood realizing that they can do whatever they want. In this moment in history, particularly in the US, we're the authors of our own lives. I work every day to provide that example for them. I hope it takes hold for them earlier than it did for me.

Grim
Determination

Tara Taylor woke up in mid-life, a bit like I did. We met in 2004, when she was in her late forties. I was looking to fill a marketing job on my staff, and she had been one of about 100 applicants for the position.

Tara was smart, poised, thoughtful, and articulate. Of the half dozen candidates I interviewed, she was my top choice. I offered her the job. A few days later, she turned it down so she could accept another position at half the salary, working in public radio. This was among the early steps in her declaration of independence from the lifetime of determination, hard work, and sacrifice that she inherited from her father.

Tara's father Neil was born in Scotland in 1925, and grew up there during the Depression and World War II. As Tara sees it, one of the drivers for her father was an utter fear of poverty, because he had grown up in its grasp. His home was a two-room flat, with a movable tub for bathing. The family took in boarders during the summer to earn extra money.

Neil studied engineering because, Tara said, it kept him from being drafted and going to war. "The reason this is relevant is that he always told me, 'Study what you love.' Because he was not allowed to study what he loved, and he really wanted to be a veterinarian." He

121

graduated at twenty from a technical college and worked all over the world as a civil engineer for Wimpey, an international construction firm.

Tara's father met a woman in Singapore whom he married in 1954, when both were in their late twenties. They came to the US and Neil took a job with Bechtel, where he worked for 30 years. Tara was born in Oxnard, California in 1958, the second of three children. Her father shaped his children through his seriousness and the intensity he brought to his work.

"The person my father was before I was born was very different than the one I knew growing up," Tara said. "My aunt and uncle tell me my father was very lively and liked to go out and have a good time. And the father I knew wasn't like that. He was very serious, undemonstrative, and reserved.

"As I was growing up, my dad worked all the time. He was a workaholic. Most days, my father was gone before we got up in the morning and he usually came home about 6:30, and sometimes he worked after dinner. And he typically did not take any vacations with us because he felt that he couldn't be away from work.

"My parents never had people over. They had one couple they played bridge with but I'm thinking, even as a child, where's the joy? Where's the laughter? It wasn't part of their lives. I think it was there at some point, but it went away long before I can really remember."

Her father had open heart surgery twice, the first time at 47. After his first surgery, he missed work for nearly four months and didn't use up all his sick leave.

"I realized when I was about ten or eleven years old that he had an addiction of sorts to work. I remember my parents were looking to buy a new house, and I couldn't understand why they would buy a new house, because then you won't have any money to go out and enjoy your life. There was money, and everything was all right, but it was just this mindset.

"At home on the weekends, the joke was, 'Why hire someone to help with the gardening or whatever because we have three kids?' So we grew up very focused on work. My mother grew up in the Depression, too, so they both were very serious, hard-working people. I learned how to work and I can focus like nobody's business and have been able to all the way through school, with just the power to concentrate and work and get something done. The other side that I had to learn as an adult is the joy part, stopping along the way to have fun.

"My older brother and I grew up waiting for our parents to get divorced. They didn't necessarily fight all the time, but it's just this tension in the house that you wouldn't want to set Dad off because he was so stressed from work. So I learned to hide who I was, because I didn't want anything to come out that was controversial, that might set off my father. It's almost the dynamic of an alcoholic family, only no one was an alcoholic."

I wondered who that young girl was who decided to shut down. She was, Tara said, "creative, and expressive, loving, and affectionate. I think often I would have become an artist. I would have just tried more things. I would have had more confidence."

At the same time Tara was shutting down emotionally, her father was becoming more emotionally distant. "When I started to develop, when I was eleven or twelve, my father said, 'I can no longer hold your hand.' And I don't know if this goes back to the old country and you want to be completely above board, but he was very mindful of that. I tell my brother who has two daughters, 'Hug your daughters no matter how old they are. Let them always feel comfortable with your physical presence because it's so important to be a safe, loving man for your girls.'

"I remember my father hugging me twice in my life. Once my brother and I were in seventh or eighth grade and we had gone with some friends to the beach, and we came home and my dad hugged me. Then the next time was the last time I saw him. He walked across the room and hugged me and told me he loved me. I was 24. I didn't know what was going on but it was so out of character that I realized afterwards he was saying goodbye. After he did die, I knew that, okay, that's what that was. He died in 1983. He was 58 and I was 25.

"One of the things that comes out of that history is that I would assume that someone loved me whenever they showed me any physical affection. I couldn't discern until well into adulthood that just because someone wants to sleep with you doesn't mean they love you. I associated physical touch with, 'This person loves me,' because I so craved warmth and affection.

"I would get involved with men who were very remote. That felt familiar. That was my pattern. The other thing was that I would work everything to death. I would just keep on working it like solving a problem and it's all focused on the other person instead of, 'What do I really want?' I didn't ask, 'What's in it for me?' until my early forties.

"I went on and got my bachelor's in art history. I didn't have enough confidence to actually create on a canvas, so I studied art history, and then I got an MBA. With an MBA I was in environments where people work all the time. So the kind of education I pursued and the environment I put myself in was very much those workaholic types of environments.

"But that never meshed with who I was internally. So it was always a rub. Part of me is in these workaholic environments but that doesn't fit with who I really am. And it's not that I don't work hard but I was thinking, 'Gosh, don't those people want to go home?' It was just always startling to me, like, 'Don't you have families and things you want to do?'

Tara and I talked as well about those aspects of her family life that were functional and helpful. She said there were plenty. "The greatest blessing my father gave me was his extended family. My mom was estranged from her father, her mother committed suicide, her brother never married. But my father has this big extended family in Britain who I met for the first time when I was sixteen. I go over and see them every two or three years, and when I go there, it has always felt like home in a way that the US never has.

"My father has an older brother, and I'm closer to him than I ever was to my father, even if I only see him every two, three years. And so I thank God every day for both my father's extended family and this sense of roots, and also for my brothers. I never questioned that my father really loved me, but it's like somebody you can't reach, you can't connect with."

Tara said she also received from her father the benefit of his wisdom to study what you love. "I heard that, but it took me years to really act on it. My strength, my ability to focus, comes from my father. Despite his remoteness, I knew he always loved me and he was a very, very kind man.

"Do what you love. Listen to your gut. And I do that well now that I had to go through my own life lessons. Here's the most profound example: I was engaged to someone when I was in Denver. And then I broke it off and came here. I had quit my job and sold my townhouse and moved here without a job at 45 years old. And I knew it would be okay because it was the first time that I really said, 'I'm gonna do what I want, I'm gonna do what I love, and I'll listen to it.'

"I was in a relationship that I wasn't happy with and I could have solved the financial problems by living with my fiancé. But I didn't want to live with him. The other dynamic was getting fired without severance. Bad, bad vortex of stuff happening. And I remember being in the counselor's office: 'What am I going to do? I don't want to live with my boyfriend but he could move in with me, pay the mortgage, he makes a nice comfortable six figures.' And my therapist said, 'Well, what would your dad tell you to do?' And I said, 'Well, he would tell me to sell my townhouse and get on with it. He would say, 'Just get on with it. It's only a house.'

"And that was such a clear voice; it was my dad speaking to me. 'You have the money, it's there.' So I sold it and I left Denver and my life began at 45. And I have never looked back. But it was the wildest thing, this clarity that said, 'Just be done with it.' And it just came out: 'Just be done with it.'

"It was almost like a religious experience. So I moved here, and the energy that came with doing that has been profound. Because the life I have now is the life I always wanted to have but could never get to. And I thank God every day that I have this second life. I'm at a place I love with people I love. I'm not trying to live anyone else's life. I'm not trying to make a relationship work that's not for me. I'm not in a corporation because I think that's where I should be.

"I'm so grateful for the opportunities I've had since then. I remember that every day. So how does that tie to my father? You just work the problem. I figured, 'There's jobs you do for career and there's jobs you do for cash. I can clean houses. And I can go try to find a better job.'

"So it's like my father's spirit gets internalized in a different way. It's your spirit as a father that your children will come back to, and that's what they carry with them. And you continue to set that example. The sad thing for me is I always wanted to be close to my dad and it wasn't meant to be."

When Tara and I met for our interview she was 52. Her father had been dead for 26 years. When I asked if she missed her father, and what she wished they could do over together, she told me, "I don't know, because I didn't know him that well. I would like to have known him, and I'm sorry I didn't know him that well. I've gotten to know my father through other people, more than first-hand experience. I know Dad through my brother, and through his brother and his sister. I know him more figuratively.

"I wish we'd had more time just to have fun. More time to go for a hike, you know, go to the zoo, just more one-on-one time. I think I just would have liked to have his attention, have his counsel, his focus. That's so precious. There's so much to be done in life maintenance that it's important just to take the time to let your children know that they matter.

"The other thing, I never felt he was happy. And maybe if you asked him he would have said he was, but I don't think he was a happy man. And I wish he had been. I just wish there'd been more joy in his life. The only thing I saw that really brought him joy was the dog."

What Tara said next struck me in how I think about my relationship with my own daughters, and what is realistic to expect from them, as their father. "You don't see your parents as people, you see them as parents first and so you expect more of them than you do anybody else. And you have expectations of them that nobody can fulfill. But you don't understand that until you're way into adulthood. And then you see that they were just struggling with their own things."

Tragedy's
Aftershocks

Diana contacted me in response to some online recruiting I did in the early months of my work. A medical doctor, she also holds a PhD in nutrition. At 43, she was married and taking time off from her career to raise her son when we became acquainted.

Before our interview, we met for coffee and I could feel there had been hard corners in her life. I had no idea how hard. Raised in New Jersey, Diana was born into a family that was profoundly shaken when the parents took a day trip to Atlantic City, leaving her siblings with their grandparents.

Diana's father Andrew is the eldest of three boys, born in Jersey City to two immigrants from Lutz, Poland. His parents came to the US when they were fifteen years old in 1914. Andrew's father and uncles worked for the New York Telephone Company as carpenters until they saved enough money to start their own hardware and lumber store in New Jersey.

Andrew was born in 1926 and began working in the family store at thirteen. He later joined the Coast Guard during the Korean War and was stationed off the Florida coast. Following his service, he attended the University of Florida at Jacksonville on the GI Bill.

After graduating with a degree in business administration, he returned to the family store, marrying the bookkeeper in 1950. He was 39 when Diana was born in the back yard of their Englewood, New Jersey home on Labor Day. Her mother, who was in labor for 26 minutes, was in a kiddie pool with Diana's sister. "The doctor got there in time to deliver me," Diana said. "And then we were brought to the hospital. From that point on, I was always itching to get out into the world.

"I've always been sort of outsider-ish of the family. I'm the only one west of the Hudson River. No one else is blonde. There is no one else with blue eyes. My sister and my mom are very different than I am in terms of how they relate to one another and the world. I've always tried to minimize trouble, or being in the way in my family, trying to stay out of people's way."

Diana's pursuit of harmony has its roots in a family tragedy before she was born, when her parents had taken a day off to go to the beach by themselves. Her older brother Adrian, who was nine, and seven-year-old sister Denise, were staying with their grandmother. As they were walking home from school a drunk driver ran over and killed Denise.

"My parents have never come to terms with it. My father has been able to, in the sense that he's just a lot better at packing luggage and putting it away. He finds compartments. And he's able to do it in a way that it seems to not be right below the surface like with my mom. She has been unable to tear this pain from every single compartment of her life.

"My brother felt that he should have been the one to die. He totally, truly felt responsible for her death. From the time he was about eleven, he was getting expelled from school. Immediately my parents had two daughters—my sister and me—so there's my brother needing someone to deal with the grieving process, in his vulnerable years, and there's my mom trying to take care of newborn babies and my dad working in the shop seven days a week. When my brother was eighteen, he was already on heroin. He went to Woodstock and he stayed away for two years.

"I am told by my aunt and others that my mom changed forever. My only experience of her has always been that she's somewhat neurotic. And I've found it hard to predict what comforts her and what doesn't, and I don't really understand her.

"So my sister was there to be a replacement child for Denise, and my brother was a whole 'nother book. When my sister, Denise, died he was told by my mother and father never to mention her name again. Every picture was taken down of her."

Diana's father dealt with his daughter's death "the way he deals with life in general," she said. "That is, he works seven days a week. Every day my dad would get up and have his own breakfast, and be gone by the time we were going to school. He would be home around six and we'd all have dinner, then he would go into his office and do his bills.

"It certainly drew my mother and father closer. They are extremely close and have an extremely loving and romantic relationship. They've been married for over 57 years. But he seems wrought with guilt. My dad has not lost his range of emotionality, including pain. He's comfortable expressing pain, remorse, crying in public, expressing feelings of guilt, sadness, happiness, all of them.

"From an early age, I recognized my dad is someone I can talk to. I started working and doing whatever I could do to help, counting nails, since I was eight years old. And before that I was playing hide and seek in the lumber yard and getting rides on the forklift. I spent all my time not in school or homework at the store. It was a second home to me."

Diana's earliest memory of her father is when he took her, as a very young girl, to his high school to show how blacks had been treated there. "There was a separate water fountain in the back. And it was scratched out but you could see it: Colored. And I was sick. My father wanted to hone that in. It was very meaningful. I think it probably was a symbol of what victimhood can be, and how people can victimize others. And how one needs to command presence and overcome and fight."

Another early memory was her father teaching her to drive—when she was six. "His constant expectation of me was to do things that I felt I was never expected to be capable of. So teaching me to drive, telling me about these inequities in life, and expecting me to sort of push my way through things. I never articulated it at the time, but I kept thinking, 'Why is he telling the little blonde cute fool these things?'"

When she reflects on her childhood, Diana recalls it as "pretty miserable with the exception of the scent of fresh pine and cedar. I know all my wood. The only joy I can recall from childhood was the scent of wood and also the rail yard that would deliver the lumber. And I used to stare at the cars and count them and fantasize about jumping on a car and running away.

"My mother was abusive physically with me. My sister was much bigger than me and so I don't know whether it was the dynamics of the relationship or the physical differences, or perhaps there were resemblances between me and Denise, I don't know. But my mother never abused my sister and my mother and sister always had a rapport. I had been beaten so badly that by the time I was in second grade my drug-addicted brother was calling the police. I had a black and blue eye because I was late for a ballet class or something.

"And my father was very much an absent player in all this. And I resent him for it and I've told him that I've felt significant anger for that. And unlike my mother who has denied that it ever existed, despite police reports, my father is able to acknowledge it, and has broken down into tears extensively. He's apologized profusely and also recognized and acknowledged with me full circle the extent of neglect that allowed that to occur.

"My father gave me a job; I worked at the store once I was sixteen. So he tried to take me away from that environment in the only way he knew, I guess. I really feel that my father saved me as best he could, which was to extricate me from my mother by bringing me to work and showing me that I'm capable of being a contributing, thinking, bright person, not the cute blonde baby. And so that's what he did for me. And I think if somebody hadn't done that for me, over the years while I was forming my identity, I don't think I could have ever taken myself seriously.

"I got into Columbia undergrad, but they wouldn't pay because they said that I was not serious enough about education or academics. It took ten years for me to convince myself that my parents were not right about everything and that I did have something academically and that my blonde hair and my passivity with regard to Mom's abusive-aggressive style was not a reflection on my own inability to think or comprehend."

Diana took it upon herself to unravel the pain and damage of her upbringing. She spent eight years in intensive therapy, seeing a psychoanalyst three times a week. "It was very difficult. I paid for that. My parents have never paid for housing, food, wedding, anything. I was very angry, obviously, up until adulthood and therapy. I learned so much about myself and my family. It really helped me develop a context in which I could actually form bonds as I did with my father that helped me really to this day in coping.

"There are limits to what I can do with my family. I don't have any problems with my dad, except for his lack of intervention, which we've discussed repeatedly. When my son was born, my father couldn't talk, he just burst into tears when I called and told them. He was so overjoyed."

Diana has been by her father's side, figuratively, since then. He worked until he was 82 and then developed cancer. That was followed by a car accident, then a severe heart attack.

"At the hospital they said to make plans for his funeral, and I said, 'Fuck you. Get me the most aggressive, gung ho cardiothoracic surgeon available. I know you know 82-year-olds, but I know my father. My father wants to live. My father will make it if you get a surgeon to repair his aortic valve. And he'll actually go back to work.' That's the bond that my father and I have. My father's got the fight. And it's the fight that he fought, that I fight, that bonds us.

"They may look at an 82-year-old male on a ventilator who's just finished rounds of chemotherapy and has lymphoma, and all normal sense would say, 'Let's get the family set so they understand the severity.' But I just knew.

"My father knows that I fought for him. I have this bitchy—if I were a man I guess it would be called stern—spirit. I did it in front of everybody when they were talking about funeral plans. I told them to all fuck off. Growing up in a lumberyard with contractors in New Jersey, your language skills, no matter how many years of advanced education you have, you still seem to have a gutter mouth. So I told my mother and my sister to fuck off because this is an arena in which I have expertise that they do not. And they can hate me forever but now they need to shut up and let me run his cardiac team. They were very difficult, but my father's sister told them to shut up and listen to me. And they did.

"I don't even know exactly what it was inside that pushed me. But somehow I was on the phone between the cardiologist and his pulmonologist and the critical care doc and the surgeon. And they all concurred with me that my dad absolutely is not the person that you take off the ventilator, because they'd known him for 30 years. And they knew he was not ready to go anywhere.

"When I came home, there were messages on my answering machine and emails from my sister thanking me. First time in my life, ever. Thanking me for fighting and for taking the helm. And that they didn't realize how much I could do."

I asked Diana if her tenacity came from her father. She said it did in a roundabout sense. "I think I did it in response to the lack of my father's doing it. Growing up, my father could have been a protector, but he wasn't. He was an avoider. And I've always been confrontational. Which is like the worst possible thing my family could tolerate. When they're trying to put something underneath the table, I'm taking the tablecloth off and saying, 'What is that?' and it just kills them."

Like many other women I spoke with, Diana was profoundly shaped by her father's immersion in his work. "The reason that I didn't get married until a few years ago and have a son until two years ago is because my father was my role model. And his whole life was work. In my mind, once I found something that I was passionate about, I felt completed by having a life totally submerged in my work. I feel that my work is a very significant contribution to the world. I don't think that's a sort of spirit or a perspective that a lot of women take. That is something that my father really taught me through modeling.

"That was something I saw him do. And I saw him happy, and I saw him capable of emotionality which to me seems like a really healthy piece of a person. And it's through that that I think I found love and marriage and a child. And found the confidence to actually step away from that daily work grind to enjoy my son for a while and not lose confidence and not lose my identity as a professional.

"I think the impact he's had on me has maybe made relationships with men a little bit unusual for me. I think a lot of men may find my personality not what they were expecting. I'm too assertive. I guess a little bit contradictory. Physically I have a very feminine persona but it doesn't in any way detract from what some people believe to be masculine traits."

Diana's turning point with her father occurred when she was 25. While she was in therapy, her analyst asked that Diana's parents come for a session. They did, and during that session, she said, her father broke down. "There were floods of tears. And through his tears he discussed how he spent so much time at work that he pigeonholed me into a role. And it was from that point onward that my father and I began talking more about our relationship. That was the first time I saw my father cry.

"It was a change point, an absolute pendulum switch. Because it suddenly clicked in me that it wasn't all me, and it didn't have to be about anger. There were much deeper issues and that we both sort of shared a certain responsibility, me as an adult to move on and be responsible for owning my own life and him for acknowledging sentiments that I had had for so long. It meant so much to me.

"And it was enough to spur me on, to feel that maybe not everybody sees me through the lens that I thought my family saw me through. Maybe they did have their own issues. My father was willing to affirm that. And I guess I needed it. Or at least it certainly helped. That was a big change point for me as an adult. It brought my father and I closer, and initiated a new relationship as adults."

I found something in Diana's story that played out with other women, and that I touched upon only briefly in "The Long Straw" section. It's how she, and several other women, established adult-adult relationships with their fathers. Those relationships were redefined during an epiphany that the daughter has that comes from her father's opening himself emotionally.

When daughters see their fathers struggling or in pain, they come to see them as people, not just as parents. This insight came to Wendy, when she walked into her father's office and saw the parenting books he was studying. Jeanne Zucker remembered the breakthrough when she saw her father cry when they visited Auschwitz in his eighties. And Mariah Castle, the actress, came to know her father through his openly sharing his stories of rejection, loss, and grief.

I've come to think that this kind of authenticity and emotional availability to their daughters may be the only way for fathers to become truly known to their daughters. Daughters don't know their fathers as employees, bosses, husbands, co-workers, brothers, sons, friends, client reps, survivors of abuse, or any of the dozens of roles their fathers occupy. Instead, they know their fathers one-dimensionally.

I think it's through authenticity, humility, and openness that fathers actually find the joy of adult relationships with their daughters. The breakthrough happens when fathers peel off the hard shells they wore as family providers and protectors and let their daughters see what's inside, including their own pain and heartbreak.

I wish there were an easier way. But I don't think there is.

Do As I Say

I met Sindhu shortly after she and her husband moved to the US from London, and asked her if she would join me for an interview. Born in Bangalore, India in 1976, Sindhu eagerly accepted my offer.

As I sat with her and listened to her story, I marveled at the profound role that arranged marriages play in the lives of millions of women around the world. I couldn't help but wonder about the role that fathers play in laying down an emotional imprint for later romantic attraction that their daughters feel toward some men and not others—and how that blueprint for attraction gets ignored when a woman's marriage partner is chosen by her parents.

Sindhu's father Sriram was born in 1947, the year of Indian independence, in a small village in Karnataka state. He was the youngest of eight children, raised primarily by his mother after his father became paralyzed on one side when Sriram was about three years old. "She instilled in all her children that education is the most important thing, you need to do well in school and only then you can progress in life," Sindhu said.

Her father was shaped by that lesson, and earned scholarships through college and graduate school during the 1960s in the US, studying mechanical engineering. "He really enjoyed living in the US," Sindhu said. "It opened up a whole new world, the way things are done here. He got a job in Chicago and then he went back to India to get married."

Marrying in India was less a matter of courtship and more a matter of parental dictation. And with Sriram's American education he was seen as a desirable husband by the parents of most young women. "In those days," Sindhu explained, "somebody returning from the US, the parents of the girl would just say yes without even meeting the boy, because it was very prestigious and your daughters could have a very good life going to the US. So, obviously, my mother's family was very excited. And then they met. And meeting is just the families talking and basically looking at each other and you have to say yes or no and that's it. But my father was like, 'No, I need to talk to her.'

"They went upstairs and spoke for like four or five hours. My dad told my mother about America, the life here and asked her what she would like to do, would she like to stay home or would she like to study further or what her plans were. He was very open about how much he made and how much he saved and what his future plans were regarding work and children. He laid out the whole thing and was like, 'So, what do you think?'

"They got married within a week after they met, because my father had to come back to America to get back to his job. But when my father came back to the US, he wasn't allowed to enter the country, because he had accidentally overstayed his work permit by a week."

Sriram returned to India and, with virtually no money left, reapplied for a visa and waited for a response. "Every evening, he and my mother would go out and walk all the way to the temple and buy a bag of peanuts and walk back. My mother says that was the most romantic time of her life, because they had no money and still they enjoyed each other's company so much.

"While he was trying to get back to the US, he had a chance to go to Iran. He likes to travel, so he said, 'Why not?' His sister lived there and the money was good. So they lived in Iran for three years."

In 1979, three years after Sindhu was born, she and her mother left Iran as the revolution erupted. "My dad put us on the last plane out and then all of Khomeini's supporters closed down the airport, because they didn't want the Shah's supporters to leave. My father was stuck. He took the land road from Iran and came through Afghanistan and Pakistan back to India. A few months after that, we moved to Kuwait. We stayed there until we came back to India in 1990 for my cousin's wedding, and then my dad returned to Kuwait."

Sindhu was one of the women I interviewed who clearly remembered the attachment and affection she felt for her father while she was growing up. "I loved him very much. I was also very scared of disappointing him. He did so much for us, and the only way I could make him happy was by doing well at school. He sent me to all these different classes, the music and the dance and I used to swim every evening. He wanted me to be busy all the time learning things. I excelled at everything I did, mainly because I wanted to please him. Whether I was interested in it or not was secondary."

This emphasis on achievement came at a cost, however. "I never had time to play, because he had me in all these different classes that went from after school into the evening. I wasn't allowed to watch TV, and he discouraged me from having friends. Friends were a waste of time and friends took you away from learning.

"I was very introverted until I came to India. When we would go to a party, I would take some books and sit in a corner and read while all the other children were playing. I never thought it was abnormal. My mother would say, 'Why don't you go and play?' But my father would say, 'Let her read.'"

From her mid-teens through her mid-twenties, Sindhu lived apart from her father. "He got a job in Bahrain for a year. Then his old company in Kuwait contacted him after the war, and he worked for them for another few years. My mother, sister, and I lived in India during that time. He would visit us twice a year. He's very family oriented, so it was hard for him. But he felt that he should provide for us, and he couldn't make any money living in India.

"It was not a good age to be away from him, because he was the main influence in my life. He would lay out all the rules and we would follow them, even the classes we went to. He was very particular about studying. He expected that I should always score 100 in math. Math was his favorite subject and he taught me. He would sit with me while I was studying and he was working, and if I had any questions, I could just ask him right away and get it solved. That was the routine every evening.

"I liked it. When I came back to India from Kuwait, I had to study independently and that became so difficult, because I was so used to having him next to me all the time, and getting myself to actually sit and study was difficult. I missed having him there. Also, that fear of disappointing him reduced a bit, because he was not there physically. So I didn't do as well as I did earlier; I was not as serious about studying as I was in Kuwait. I wish he had let me develop my own pattern of studying and let me study on my own."

While her father wasn't with her physically, Sindhu said, he still was able to exert his influence. "It's not that he didn't have an influence over me. He did. We used to write fairly long letters to each other every few months. And my dad had a few special sayings. 'Hard work pays and laziness destroys.' Also he said, 'Time is of the essence. You'll never get your time back, so use it wisely.' And 'You should always keep learning. There's so much to learn in life.'

"By the time I was sixteen, I realized that probably everything that my dad says is not applicable. Like, things are very different from when he was younger. It was a difficult time, because my mother would tell me to do things and I would be like, 'No, I want to do something else.' She was, of course, very surprised and very scared, because she's like, 'I'm losing control over my daughter.'

"My dad was like, 'You just need to obey your mother without asking any questions. We obeyed our mother and we are all successful.' So I could never argue with my dad. I could only argue with my mother, which is sad, because she had to bear the brunt of it."

I asked why she felt she couldn't argue with her dad. "Maybe because I was still scared of disappointing him or maybe I didn't want him to think that I didn't respect him. And I don't know, with my mom, I guess I had to take out all the frustration on somebody. And, see, with my dad, he would just say statements like, 'We did what our mother wanted and look where all of us are. So you need to do the same thing.' And I couldn't argue with that, because, yes, they were all successful."

Despite the geographic separation between himself and his daughter, Sriram never let up on his fathering. The letters, Sindhu recalls, were "basically a repetition of what he would say over the phone. It would be complaints from my mother that I wasn't obeying her. He would write about how children often think that they know what the right thing is, but they don't. And parents do, because we are older, more experienced and we have seen the world. You did well this time, but you could do better. So it was always, 'It was not good enough. You could do better.'

With her father's constant prodding from afar, Sindhu excelled academically, and was accepted into medical school. But that, too, was something her father chose. "By the time I was eighteen, I knew what I wanted to do and what I really loved, English and history. My other choice was a PhD in math. I had my misgivings about medical school. I quickly realized that it was not what I wanted. I didn't know how to make the right decisions for myself. I was never trained to think. It was just like, 'Do this,' and you do it and you do your best.

"I really wish my father had taught me to think and weigh pros and cons and investigate things before making a decision, because my parents would do all that. So I never had an opportunity to do that for myself. Because of that background, I made mistakes at crucial times, like getting into medical school, getting married to the wrong person—these were big mistakes.

"From my dad, I did learn to be open, and say what I meant, but with other people, not with my parents. Isn't that funny? But after I got into medical school, my dad started treating me like an adult, so I could start discussing things with him. I guess it was, again, the American influence; eighteen, you're an adult. And I think it was because I had achieved that ambition of his, I'd done everything expected of me, so now he would treat me as an adult. He started discussing everything. Now he discusses everything with me, all his investments and financial matters. He wanted me to know, in case anything happened to him. And since my mother was not interested in that side of things, he decided to tell me."

Even though he began treating Sindhu more like an adult, Sriram had one enormous task remaining as a father: Finding his daughter a suitable husband. "Mine was an arranged marriage; my ex-husband came to the US for his master's degree and was working here. My father put a matrimonial ad in the paper and his father responded. Then our families met and I started talking to my ex over the phone.

"I didn't feel pressured to marry *him*, but I felt pressure to get married, because I was 25 and that is late for Indian girls. My father was worried that my choices will be slim, because all the eligible grooms, who would be around maybe 29, 30, would all be married.

"I got married there and we came over to Phoenix, because that's where my first husband lived. My dad always used to tell us that America's the place to live. I started going to school the day after I got here to the States. I had finished medical school in India, and then in Phoenix I studied computer information systems and worked for a hospital in their IT department."

Sindhu had a model from her parents for how an arranged marriage could become romantic. "He used to send her greeting cards, for Valentine's and for her birthday and for the anniversary, these really huge beautiful ones, with roses and all these really nice words. And if they'd go to a store and my mother would pick something up and say, 'Oh, this looks nice,' he would just buy it for her right away. So that was what I saw growing up, and that was how I thought.

"My dad always said, 'There's no such thing as love before marriage. It only comes after you get married, because that's a commitment, and you eventually fall in love with your husband or wife. Before you marry, it's infatuation. And boys get attracted to anything in a sari. So you shouldn't take anyone seriously if they tell you they love you, because it's just infatuation.'"

The marriage that was arranged for Sindhu wasn't anything like her parents'. After seven years, and with a nine-month old son, she decided to end the relationship. Her father supported her decision. "When I called and told him, 'I've decided I'm going to get divorced. This is just not working out,' he said, 'All right, do you need anything?'"

A year later, Sindhu was ready for a serious relationship. "There's an Indian matrimony website now. So I put up my profile, and I came across my current husband's profile, and we started talking. I told my father, 'I've started talking to this guy. He's also from Bangalore.' And he said, 'Oh, good. Let me know when you meet him.'

Sindhu and her son moved to London, where her future husband lived, in July of 2008. In November they went to Vegas and got married. "It was such an easy wedding, fifteen minutes and we were married. So I ended up doing what I had wanted to do. I wanted to meet someone on my own, date, fall in love, and get married in Vegas."

I then asked Sindhu which of her parents she thought was more influential on who she has become. "My father, definitely, definitely, because after eighteen, I could start expressing myself with him, little by little. With my mother, I never could.

"In so many things, he was very modern. 'You need to be educated. You need to be independent. You have to learn to drive.' But, at the same time, he was very traditional when it came to marriage. When I got married the first time, he said, 'You have to do whatever your husband says for the first three years, and then he will start listening to you.'

"I thought if I do what he says, I'm going to be miserable forever. And his thinking was so contradictory. On one side, he wanted his daughters to be independent and educated and earn for themselves.

And on the other hand, he wanted us to be the docile housewives with the husbands. I don't know how that could work."

Not being good enough is another belief that stuck with Sindhu. "Even now, I was just learning a new song on the violin that I'll be playing with a group this weekend. I practiced it today and my husband came into the room and said, 'That was very good,' and I was like, 'No, it's not. It's not good enough.' And he's like, 'Don't get upset. It sounded nice.' And I said, 'No, it has to be better.'"

That, Sindhu acknowledged, was her father's tape running inside of her mind. "Yeah, yeah, it has to be better, it has to be perfect. I'm like that with other things, too, with the house, the way things should be kept. It really gets me upset if things are not done the way they should be done. I try my best and sometimes I feel disappointed if things are not done perfectly. My current husband is so relaxed, like, 'Do whatever makes you happy.' I say I feel he should tell me what to do, because I'm so used to that. He's like, 'No, you decide for yourself.'

"I still haven't become totally assertive. He said, 'I'll respect you more if you're assertive. You just have to learn to say no, and you shouldn't think that you're disappointing people who love you.' So, it's the pattern. It's still there."

The solitude her father encouraged, as a path to achievement, is still there in some measure for Sindhu. "I definitely would have liked my dad to let me interact with other people. That would have helped me evolve better. I wish he had been more open about boys, so I would have learned to think of them as just another human being, not something forbidden or dangerous or I'm not supposed to talk to at all. Definitely, the social aspect was missing and I think that would have made a big difference. And I wish he had helped me through decision-making. Because halfway through medical school, when he visited India, I told him, 'I don't want to do this,' and he said, 'Okay, let's sit down and write down the pros and cons.'

"So he made, like, two columns and he wrote down everything.

And I was like, 'I wish he had taught me to do this earlier,' so that it would help me make good decisions, because good decision-making is so much more important than scoring 100 in math.

"It happens with most children from Asian countries, because the importance is given only to education and you are expected to obey. So decision-making is very difficult for us. I think dads should teach their daughters how to think and how to decide and how to problem solve. Especially when it comes to relationships, because you can meet the wrong kind of guy, and that can just ruin your life. And I think dads need to tell their daughters, 'If you meet somebody who you think is great and you get married and you feel it doesn't work out within a certain span of time and there are things that just cannot change, don't stay, don't ruin the rest of your life.'

"My father was like, 'Okay, you've tried and that's it,' because he knew that I'd tried. I really had. I really am thankful to him for that, because if he had told me to stay and if he didn't support me, then it would have really been so difficult.

"He has also taught me how to be a very dedicated parent. So when my current husband does things for my son, it reminds me of my father. So, I ended up marrying a man who is so much like my father in many ways, but more modern thinking, more open."

An Emotional Wall
of China

Sometimes the world seems small. I've worked with Mei at two separate companies, and with her husband at another. She was 37 and working in the finance department of a high tech firm when we met for our interview.

Mei's father Chen was born in 1946 in Beijing, China to parents who were in their late forties, and whose other biological children had all died young. He grew up, Mei said, essentially as an only child, even though he had an older sister whom his parents had adopted before he was born. "Basically, my father got all the undivided attention and he was everything to them. I was told he was totally spoiled and didn't have to do anything in the house."

After graduating from high school, Chen went to work as an elementary school physical education teacher, then moved on to a factory doing research before ultimately managing the business. Mei was born and raised in China, then came to the US in her mid-twenties.

Early in our conversation, as we talked about her father, Mei had a revelation: "It's kind of dawned to me that I don't really know a whole lot about my father. I never took the time to learn about what's going on in his life," she said. "It's just the unfortunate reality.

"I think my dad is a caring person. But for some reason I just never took the time to get close to him. I think it's because when I was young, he liked to go out to soccer games and to watch hockey games and he would come home very late. And he liked to hang out with his friends, go out to dinner. He likes to socialize. He likes to go out and do things. So if anyone from work said, 'Hey, let's have a beer after work,' he would be there. He wouldn't be home.

"Whenever there's a chance to go hiking, go and play basketball, go swimming, he would do it. I think he just didn't realize when you have kids, your life changed. He has this enormous interest in a lot of things and he didn't learn to give up those when he had me. And my mother was left with me. There was some resentment from my mother. It's kind of sad. I think my mom had all the right reason to complain. I can't imagine me marrying someone who's just rarely around. He just did things he was interested in. He wasn't prepared for his role of father or husband."

Like Hana, Mei doesn't recall a childhood infatuation with her father. "I don't think I have a really warm fuzzy feeling towards him. I never had that. It's kind of surprising to realize it, because I never give it much thought. It's just the way it is. I think in a way it's because my father was unavailable a lot.

"When I was in junior high, high school, college, the three of us went out every weekend to shopping, to parks, to dinner, and we traveled a little bit together. But I never had that strong bond with him or much close interaction. He drove me to school a lot when I went to college. That was the time I had alone with him. But I never really felt comfortable. It felt like, 'Oh, I wish someone else was driving me to school.' So many times, there was just silence between us in the car. I didn't know what to talk about. And he probably wasn't comfortable with me.

"Growing up, I don't think there is any particular thing that we did together. Usually it was the three of us, or me and my mother. Maybe my mother was too available, so my dad couldn't compete with her. Now, when thinking about it, I feel sad. But in the past, I never felt that way. I assumed that's the way it should be.

"Since he retired, he has been to the States a few times. Now, he's with us. I feel like our relationship has improved, especially seeing how much he loves and adores my daughter, and how much he takes care of her. And he cooks all the time at the house, which he never did when I was young. He seems to be a different person now. Our relationship is definitely improving, because we've had more conversation with each other. I just wish that the improvement started earlier, so I could get to know him better."

We talked about her father's distance from her, and how Mei thinks it might have shaped her. "I still think I should give him good credits for working hard and for providing good life to my mother and me. I'm sure there's got to be some impact on me, how I grow up as who I am. But I don't think I can really draw the direct relationship between me and him. To me, he's more an outsider.

"I definitely get being self-centered from my dad. My dad and I are both pretty easygoing. And I'm very caring and I think he is. He has good qualities I just never uncovered. In the past, I thought the best husband should be a great provider of the family. And I couldn't name anything else but being good provider, probably because that's what my dad was."

I noticed as our conversation carried on how intensely Mei wanted her daughter to experience a different type of father, and a different family environment. Because her mother complained to Mei about her father, Mei told me she would never do that. "Even though Robert and I have disagreements, I want to make sure I don't say anything bad about him in front of my daughter, because I want her to have a perfect memory of him." She then added that she wants her daughter to grow up "knowing he's always there to support her, to love her, to spend time with her, to do everything for her."

I thought that was a tall order for any father—to create a "perfect memory" and "do everything" for his daughter. We didn't talk about it long before Mei realized she was setting her husband up for failure, to provide the life for their daughter that Mei never had growing up.

And she realized she was doing some of the same to herself.

"I do have that expectation of myself, too, to be available. Today, during dinner, I said, 'I want to be her best friend.' Robert said, 'No. You can only be a mother. You can't be your daughter's best friend.' I said, 'No. I can be. I want to be. I want to be the mother, the best friend, everything to her.'"

Our conversation, like the others, shifted to what she had learned from life with her father. The big lesson, she said, came from the regret of not getting to know him earlier. "I wish I'd never blocked him out of my life. I always try to show my interest in people, by trying to get to know them better, even though there may be signs they're not interested in my life or interested in getting to know me. But I always make at least initial effort to get to know them, because I wish I did that earlier, when I was younger.

"I think overall my relationship with my father is relatively healthy, compared to my contemporaries back in China. It seems a little abnormal here, but it's pretty normal back in China. Parents and kids are close, but in a different way from here. The parents are supposed to be respected, so they don't share a lot with the kids, are not as open as parents are here.

"Maybe there are some profound ways my dad has influenced me, but I just can't think of any. There's got to be something there."

Native Roots

I met Teresa Kim NoBear, or "TK" as she's known to her friends, through a mutual acquaintance. She is of Nez Perce ancestry on her mother's side and German on her father's. I drove to meet her on a glorious July day at her horse ranch in the Central Oregon high desert. The scene was stunning: Her custom-built log home is filled with Native American artifacts and set on several acres surrounded by mountains. As we settled in to chairs in her spacious back yard, TK told her story and the role her father played, right down to her fantasy of building the log home. She was 50 at the time of our interview.

Born in 1936, TK's father Michael was the second of five children. His mother was sixteen and his father 37 when they married. As TK tells it, her grandfather was an alcoholic who emotionally and physically abused his children.

Her dad grew up in a farming community, working in the fields and a dairy farm by day and running much of the household at night in his father's perpetual absence. When Michael was in his late teens, his father died of a heart attack. "My dad found him in the kitchen," TK said. "My aunts tell me that all he did was take care of business, go upstairs, and sit there in shock for three days."

After high school, her father worked his way from being a forklift driver into management jobs at a furniture plant. At 23, he married the woman who became TK's mother, who was 29 at the time.

As we spoke, TK described an emotionally isolated father. He came from a cultural background of German stoicism. He was raised by an abusive father with whom he could not form a close bond, and he was then traumatized by his father's death at a young age. We were still early in our conversation; I didn't yet know her story, so I asked TK if her father's emotional isolation became part of who she is. "Yes," she replied, "that does."

TK's grandmother became enraged when she learned her son was marrying a Native American woman. TK's mother heard her future mother-in-law screaming, "You can't marry her. Your children will be black. They'll be ostracized."

Undeterred, TK's parents married in 1959. TK recalls them as being "kind" but that her father in particular was emotionally distant. "He's a very nice guy. Both my parents are. He's quick to help anybody. Enough so that there was times that my mom felt like the family was the last to get help. He was a good father in terms of what he was capable of doing for jobs. He did his best to support us. My dad to this day doesn't believe in credit cards or checking accounts. They have one, but everything's cash, always has been. They bought their first home in cash."

As TK tells it, her father landed in one attractive business opportunity after another, through a combination of hard work and happy accident. He helped launch a furniture company. He started a demolition business—knowing nothing about demolition—and undercut an established group of mob-like competitors for a local dock demolition. "Dad and his partner hired a couple of kids, they tore down the dock, and then they needed a place to store this material, from timber to bricks to whatever.

"And they met two other guys that said, 'Hey, we have some property down off the Willamette River. You could just float all this stuff down there and leave it on this property.' And they eventually needed to sell that property, so my dad and his partner bought it. Then they thought, 'Why don't we just create a dock on this piece of property?' From there they developed this huge marina. They developed a string of floating docks. And now there are nearly two hundred slips down there, both covered and uncovered. And then they developed a sailboat area and a housing area."

TK has fond memories of growing up with her father, though his emotional isolation shaped the contours of how he was able to parent. "We'd go to the beach. And he seemed happy playing with me. I remember moments of watching TV, laying on the couch and watching a program with him, all through grade school. Other than that, I very seldom saw him. He was always working. He'd come straight home from work, have his dinner, watch TV, start all over again.

"The summer when I was going into sixth grade we took on playing tennis together. And then he got into jogging, so I'd run the track with him. It was fun, but it was competitive. I always felt like I had to win. We played cards a lot, too, and my dad always won. When I was in my first year of high school, we got into table tennis and we played that for hours. I do remember laughing, but I'd always be bummed because I'd lose again. And I'd say, 'Okay, Dad, let's play one more,' and we'd play 'til like ten o'clock at night and I'd go, 'No, I'm not going to bed until I win.' He never would let me win. I have that same tenacity when I take something on; I have to do it full tilt, do it the best I can."

Like many of the women I interviewed, TK wasn't starved for attention by her father, but she lacked the physical and verbal assurances of affection received by women who drew the long straw. "He was never one you could just go talk to or give a hug to. Neither one of my parents are huggable kind of people. They both stiffen up and are nervous about it."

Our conversation turned to how her father's emotional distance shaped her. She said she didn't feel neglected emotionally. "I don't think I knew any different. Not until I got a lot older. I'd go to kids' houses and I'd see they have all these grandparents and all this family and this laughter and people running up and down stairs and I was looking at it with curiosity and sometimes thought it was kind of neat.

"In some respects, I go to the opposite of my father. I'm very emotional. I find myself being very compassionate of others. I'm there to take care of others before myself. I've learned to change that, though."

I asked TK if, as a woman, she feels herself longing for an emotional connection and affection, which she experienced minimally as a girl. "I would say that's true. And at times I have to work to give that or to receive it. Especially receiving it. I get real stoic like my mom or dad. In fact I find it odd sometimes when I watch a daughter-father relationship, because there's a lot more lovingness there. They're quick to hug, kiss, sit together. And I'm like, 'That does not seem natural.' And another part of me goes, 'I wonder what that would be like.'

"I think I went through several boyfriends because of that. I made choices that were not good, because it was just somebody paying attention to me. That's a funny thing. I don't think they were comforting, even at the time, but I found myself in those relationships even knowing it wasn't right.

"When I was about sixteen, I had my first relationship with a guy that was about a year older than I was. The next relationship was with a guy who was probably at least five years older than I was. I found out later he had either a wife or another girlfriend. And then I met another character and I ended up pregnant. I told my mom I was pregnant—I was devastated, of course—and I ended up getting an abortion, and then Mom saying, 'Well, maybe you should just marry him.' I went through this whole wedding thinking it wasn't right. I was nineteen, and he was 23.

"He was an alcoholic. I remember thinking I could fix him. It became an abusive relationship to the point I would get scared at night and be half awake and half asleep, waiting for the door to come open, knowing that the anger, the drunkenness would start into a fight. I managed to get out of that relationship and I got a restraining order. And the whole time, I didn't have my parents to talk to, especially my dad. To this day, I don't even know if he knows I had an abortion. I just didn't feel I could talk to him. It was like he wasn't even there."

Our conversation turned to that inattention, and whether that may have formed some of her beliefs about men as a result. "Oh, I'm sure," she said. "Not to trust them, I need to take care of it myself. My husband and I have been married for 25 years, and there's difficulty because I just take the bull by the horns and deal with it, whatever it is."

TK didn't lack for an authority figure in her father. The best fathers I heard about during my dozens of interviews were those who knew how to provide the balance of tough love that I mentioned earlier. TK felt more of the tough than the love.

"He was definitely strict. I remember bringing home grades really excited because I got As or B-pluses or an A-minus and he'd always say, 'What's with the B, what's with the A-minus?' I remember being very frustrated by that, thinking, 'God, I still couldn't do good enough for him.' I could get straight As but there'd be that one A-minus. That would be the first thing he'd say. But I kept trying. So obviously I was still trying to get his affection and his approval. I still find myself falling into that pattern, doing things for my dad's approval.

"I remember if I got into trouble with Dad I'd get the belt. I remember running away from home in fourth grade because I was so mad at him. I hid in the woods until dark. My mom finally found me and I got in the car with her. And then I remember getting a lecture from my dad. He was so mad at me he was screaming.

"He was always the one that would force me to eat dinner. There was something I didn't like, even after I tried it, and I didn't want to eat it. But I had to sit at the table. I would sit there for as long as possible and I would refuse to eat it and he'd sit there telling me I had to and I couldn't leave the table until I did and I wasn't going to eat it. So I went to bed. And then in the morning it would be back at the table waiting for me for breakfast because I had to eat it. So I sat there and still refused to eat it until it was time to catch the bus. And if I missed the school bus I walked.

"I remember sitting on the steps one time with a friend, and I was so mad at my dad, I said, 'I just hate my dad. I hate him!' He was in the back porch, and he was listening. And he yelled, 'TERESA KIM!' I had to send my friend home. I got hauled in the house.

"When I started this ranch, I had this big dream." TK sighed and paused. "I'm gonna cry 'cause you hit a button. I remember thinking all the negativity, all the fighting that we had, we could get over that and we could work together, because my dad wanted a ranch and a cabin.

"It started with my mom. I wanted to honor her ancestry because of all that she went through, and the cabin came into play because of my dad." Then TK began to cry. "We took a walk in the woods here and I remember asking him what he wanted out of life and he said he always wanted a log cabin. So here we were.

"We were always getting into it during the whole process. He said we were spending too much money or didn't need to do that, or whatever. When I bought the ranch, I thought it would be really cool, we'd be this father and daughter working on this ranch together.

"Instead it was just a nightmare. Because I was gonna give the direction, I worked with horses, I knew how to handle horses and my dad was clueless in that respect. So when I would try to teach him, it didn't work out. Or when I had an idea of what we should repair first, it was always a fight."

There are many ways to be fathered, I've found, when a woman needs to compensate for what she didn't get growing up. Some women seek it from their husbands. Some find it in surrogates. TK is one of those fortunate women who've found surrogate fathers to help fill the hole in her heart. "I have a great relationship with my first ranch foreman, who's in his eighties, and I currently have another guy helping me and he's 78. And I guess those are the two relationships I think, 'God, that's what I really love about that, that was what I envisioned what it was like to have a real father-daughter relationship.

"They taught me a lot. I'm extremely lucky. I don't know what I would do without them. And they put joy in my life, too. They both taught me a lot in terms of relationships in general and working together. I've always had a tendency to respect and admire my elders. I felt they had the answers or wisdom. So I would seek that out, because I didn't get it at home."

Many women I interviewed could not recall their fathers telling them that they love them. TK is among those. "I don't think I've ever heard the words. My mom, yes. Not from my father. I may have a total misconception of it, but I really can't remember a time. I do know my dad loved me, and still does. But I don't remember ever being able to say, 'Okay, what do you think I should do with my life?' I figured it out on my own."

TK still feels gratitude for what her father did give her, in spite of the nurturing presence she felt was missing. She learned from her father, she said, "how to be a hard worker. How to give it your best. How to be kind to others. He and my mom were very friendly with people. There wasn't gatherings at our house much, but I remember when my dad was spending time with friends, he was in a good mood. That's when he'd laugh."

I wondered, after the hours we spent together, if TK would change anything about her past. She said she wouldn't.

"I don't really believe that if you had a choice to go back and do things that it would be necessarily for the better. We are who we are because of what we go through, good and bad. I am who I am, I'm a stronger person, I've made better decisions because of the things that I didn't necessarily have or do right back then.

"Would I have liked to have a better relationship with my dad?

Absolutely. Would I like to be able to talk to him in detail? Yes. I would love to be able to sit down and have a true, authentic conversation with my dad. We do sometimes, through books. I love to read, he loves to read. So we pass books back and forth. And we talk about those. But we both find it very difficult to talk in too much detail, especially to be intimate."

Fifteen months after our interview, TK's marriage of 25 years ended in divorce.

Her Father's Legs

Irena is a 40-year-old athlete and massage therapist from Lithuania. She has raised two sons as a single mother for much of the past fifteen years, after the death of her first husband and a divorce from her second.

We met by chance. I dropped by a clinic unannounced to ask one of my Chinese acupuncturists if she would consider an interview. She wasn't in, and I ended up talking with Irena. It didn't take me long to connect her eastern European accent to a big gap in my interview sample—I hadn't spoken yet with anyone from eastern Europe.

I asked if she'd consider doing an interview, then launched into my "This is safe" mode. As I rambled on, her warm smile slid into a look of mild impatience, until she finally cut me off. "You can stop now," she said. "I know you're safe."

We met two weeks later for our interview. That's when I came to appreciate how easily and quickly Irena can size up men. She grew up doing that, at her father's side.

Irena's father was born in Vilnius, the Lithuanian capital, in 1943. As Irena told it, his mother endured a great deal of self-inflicted shame because she had him out of wedlock. "She was so ashamed that she would ask him to call her by her name instead of Mom. My dad remembered his father until he was three, and then somehow he disappeared. He never knew what happened to him."

At five her father began having difficulty walking. By the time he finished high school, he could barely walk at all; he had multiple sclerosis. "People would think that he was drunk, and they would laugh at him if he would fall down. In Lithuania at that time, people were laughing at you if you are an invalid, if you are in a wheelchair. You are nobody. And people try to run away from you, do not look at you, or even say bad words. He felt a lot of pain from that, being not like everybody else."

By the age of 24, Irena's father was in a wheelchair. She has no memory of him walking. She does remember him drinking and smoking, in what she sees now as his attempt "to run away from himself, from his reality."

Irena's grandmother had remarried, and her husband became a father figure to Irena. "He was always very good to me. He would carry me on his shoulders. He taught me to swim. He was kind of a father with legs, because my father never could do that. And I was so jealous of those other kids whose fathers would put them on their shoulders and carry them around. I never could have that. Families would go out on vacations together. I never had that because my father couldn't."

For thirteen years Irena spent long stretches of each summer with her grandparents at the beach, taking in the physical presence of her grandfather. "I really remember that very well, because he gave to me something that I was missing from my dad. I remember he had such a big hand! I just loved that. I felt that yang power. He was in the war; he had been shot in his hand. He would tell me stories sometimes about war, how he lived through that. I just saw that strong, powerful man. I didn't have that from my dad. My dad was a more caring person, very intuitive."

Among the earliest stories Irena has of her father is his helplessness. "When I was a baby my mom needed to go to work to make money, so he was watching me. He's sitting at the edge of sofa and I'm in the cradle. He said I was kind of noisy and he's rocking me, and he leaned and fell on that handle and I flew out of the cradle on his back. He's laying on the floor with me being pretty much quiet on his back and nobody's at home. And he said, 'I cannot do anything with you.' He felt very, very disappointed that he has this little child he could not take care of.

"His friend, by accident, came by, and my dad said, 'Vitas, come over, can you help me? Is she okay?' He was very worried about me. I was fine. That was very hard on him.

"He was a very good cook. When I was maybe seven, he would sit in the chair like this, and I would drag him to the kitchen, and I would be his legs. And he would tell me what to do, what to cook. And we would make dinner."

It was Irena's next story that shed light on her ability to quickly size up men. "I remember when, in order for him to go out, I would need to go to the neighbors, and get somebody who can carry my dad downstairs from the second floor to his wheelchair. And usually he could go out just in the summertime. Usually people on Friday they leave their houses for somewhere, to the countryside, and I would not find any neighbors who can bring him upstairs.

"So when he would come back we would need to go outside on the street and wait for a guy who would walk by. And I would need to ask him to take care of my dad to bring him upstairs. And I remember I would say, 'Oh, look, there is guy,' and he'd say, 'No, no, don't go to see that guy, this is not good guy.' He would scan people before he would send me to ask for help. And it's dark, ten o'clock at night. And then he would scan somebody and be like, 'Okay, you can go ask that one.'"

Even with her father's disability, Irena said she felt protected by him somewhat. "I felt very protected emotionally, but not physically. I always thought, 'I'm very strong, I can protect myself.' But more emotionally. He was so smart, he would tell me stories and things, and I just loved listening to him. I'd say, 'Just make up a story. It doesn't need to be true. Just make up a story!' I loved that."

"I always loved him much more than my mom. My mom was a

bitch. She always yelled, she was always unhappy, she always spanked me, she always did all those bad things. I think she just was putting all that frustration, that her husband is drinking and all this work is on her shoulders, I think she just was putting it on me.

"He was protecting me from my mom. He was spending time with me. We'd play checkers, we'd play chess, we did math together. When he was playing cards with us, every time you needed to count, he would not let me to use any calculator or anything. I needed to do that in my memory. So kind of he looked for the learning process.

"Then we have these little guns, plastic dart guns. We would do things like put matches on the chair and we would shoot and see who would be the better shooter. He would read stories for me from the newspaper. We would listen to the radio together. I would love Sundays in the morning to crawl in his bed to be in between my mom and him. But more next to him."

Irena didn't love her father's smoking or drinking. She recalls that sometimes, when he was drunk, she would leave to play with her friends, and she could hear her father screaming at her mother. "When he was drunk he was very aggressive. He would throw things around. That was very embarrassing. Everybody could hear that. He wasn't the man he wanted to be or understood he needed to be.

"One time I remember my mom's friend said, 'How you can let him to call you all these names? This is emotional abuse. This is so bad. I'm going to teach him!' And she tied him with rope, and she put some stuff in his mouth that he would not scream. She physically tied him. And I remember I came home and she told me, 'You do not go and help your father. If you are going to do that, I'm going to tie you, too.'"

We talked about her father's life, his losing his own father at a young age, the harsh stepfather who took over, being laughed at for his disability, then losing his ability to take care of himself and his daughter physically, and support his family financially. In so many ways, he was stripped of his masculinity. I asked Irena if she thought her father was filled with anger and resentment, given how much of his power he had lost and the humiliation he had endured.

"Yeah, he was. I didn't see it then. However, when I look from my eyes now, I can see how it was. That's why he wanted to leave this world. Because it's so hard to live like that. That's why he was drinking.

"You know what? He gave to me that power to fight. I'm female, but I always wanted to be a boy, or I always acted like boys. I was always a fighter. And this is what I see now in me. My yang energy was always higher than my yin.

"When I started understanding my relationship with my dad, and actually now you just gave me a point, his yang was very like, they put down everything. And with me, I just picked up that I need to be yang. Because that's what my dad didn't have. So I needed to have it. So now when I start understanding this, I can just be yin, who I am."

Irena was thirteen when her father died. The loss broke her heart. "He was outside, and he never came home. I biked everywhere to look for him and I couldn't find him. I came home and my mom was like, 'Stop it, it's dark, come home.' And I said, 'I'm waiting for Dad.' Somebody called at twelve and they said about a mile away from the house that they found him dead.

"They said it was a heart attack. He was drunk. I remember I ran into that place. I came first, next to him and I took his pulse and I looked at him. He wasn't breathing and I knew that he was dead. He still was warm. My neighbor took me away from him. And then I got it. I started crying. I told my neighbor, 'I don't have my dad anymore.' I realized, this is it. I never in my life will see my dad ever again. I understood what death means." Irena began to cry. "I never, never will talk to him again, never will see him again. This is it. I don't have Dad and nobody can replace Dad ever in my life.

"Before he died I said, 'You need to be home, it's nine o'clock.' And he said, 'No, no, no, I still need to go to one place.' I said, 'No, I want you to come home.' He said 'No.' And I got mad at him. I was very mad and upset at him and called him names. And he left and he never came back alive. From that point, I learned don't ever fight with anybody. When you talk to people, finish good, do not finish bad a conversation. Because that's how I finished with my dad and I never had a chance to say I was sorry.

"After the funeral my mom sent me to this summer camp and when I came back, everything in the room was re-arranged. And I was so mad at her. I said, 'What did you do with his clothes?'"

"'Oh, there's some in the closet,' she said. And so I would sometimes put Dad's shirt on to walk around when nobody's at home. I felt that he's around me. I would go in the closet just to touch them, to look at them."

There is no good age to lose one's father. Thirteen is painfully young. Irena and her father were just beginning to enter her adolescence together.

"He was teaching me about men. If I was going somewhere, he would say, 'Remember, men want just one thing. You need to be careful. You need to stay away from men, especially from older men.' I was about eleven or twelve. Every time I leave the house I need to listen to this, and I would say, 'I know, I know, can I go now?!' And he like, 'No, you stay here and listen. This is what men want. And you are a girl. You need to stay away from them. Don't talk to them. Don't give them any reason to think about stuff. Stay away from men.'

"I never tease men, I never give men a reason to think, 'Maybe.' I'm really very straight, very clear. This is not a game. So don't even play with men. He would say, 'Don't play with fire.'

"My mom never talked to me about periods. It was my dad. My mom would say, 'I don't know what to say, you talk to her!' So when I got my period the first time I got scared, I still was like, 'Oh! What is this?' So I came to Dad and my dad said, 'Well, you're already a big girl, so your mom will show you how you need to take care of this.' Then he asked my mom to show me. And my mom said, 'No, this is not her period, she ate beet soup.' And my dad said, 'Our girl is grown up! Just get it!' He really, really loved me."

Irena's closeness with her father, combined with his disability, shaped her beliefs about a woman's role in relationship to a man: She grew up with caretaking deeply ingrained. And she paid a price for that belief. "When I was growing up, I saw a family where it's the female taking care of the man, nursing, giving, doing everything for him. So when I got married, I understood I need to take care of my man. And that is not right. It needs to be a co-creative relationship.

"For twenty years, for every man I had in my life, I was giving myself away. And my first marriage, he died. But with my second marriage I saw very clearly how I was giving away everything. And when he decided he didn't want the marriage any more, I was so bro-ken-hearted that it took me two years to get back and find my heart.

"In ten days I lost 20 pounds. I didn't eat. I would go for a 60-mile bike ride without any food. I would go for a 30-mile run. So I'd just go for five hours, six hours. I was running like a crazy woman. My heart was so broken, so broken. And that's when I started taking care of me, going for acupuncture, massage, an intuitive healer, a chi-ropractor. All my teammates helped me to build a stronger heart and understand the relationship between a woman and man is not when you're giving yourself away.

"I think my dad put a lot of influence in my life. Even though he had a lot of things to deal with, I think he was a wonderful father. And my dad, he's always with me. If I need help, I always ask him for help. He's just a spirit now, so you just talk to the spirit. If I need help with my boys, I ask my dad."

The Short Straw

Too little or no childhood closeness to an accepting father can leave a woman with various kinds of scars; insecurity is one of the deepest. Detachment is another because she does not know how to be close to a man and feels cut off...she simply does not expect love, closeness, warmth, or intimacy from a male. Anger is another unhappy legacy from this period.
William Appleton, MD
Fathers & Daughters

Life is harder for some than for others. It is also unfair.

Nowhere is this truer than among women who were abandoned or abused by their fathers, the first man in the world whose role is to protect her. As an infant and child, a daughter wants his love, admiration, and trust. Those bonds are shattered by fathers who abandon or abuse their daughters.

I was moved by the openness, honesty, and longing that writer Danielle Pergament expressed in a piece she wrote in 2011, titled, "Were You Born to Cheat?" She tells so eloquently how emotional abandonment can live on through a father and daughter.

"During the winter before my wedding, I was on assignment in Sicily, where I met Diego, a photojournalist with black hair, a scruffy beard, and warm brown eyes that could liquefy concrete. He was my guide in Palermo, driving me around the city on his motorcycle. On my last day, as we stood in a bombed-out cathedral—him talking about World War II, me trying to focus on his words—he started

169

inching closer. Another inch. Then a fraction more, and he was in my personal space. The slightest gesture from me would have been an invitation. I froze. I was madly in love with my fiancé, so what the hell was I doing?

"The desire to cheat is hardly a new emotion for me. In fact, I can fairly say that if you've dated me, there's a pretty good chance I was unfaithful. (I'm really sorry!) You might even call me a natural-born cheater—and I think I get it from my father.

"Henry Pergament was a businessman, entrepreneur and chemistry genius. By the time I was born, he'd raised several fortunes and had two families and half a dozen children in and out of wedlock. I have memories from my childhood that I wish I didn't: One night when I was about 10, I was at dinner with my sister, my father and his friend Mike. I overheard my dad say, 'What have I been up to? What men are up to when they're not with their wives.'

"Daily life in my family found my sisters, my mother and me running around the house like it was a disrupted anthill, my father somewhere off-screen. He worked hard and was often in absentia. But as I started to understand the adult world in increments, I wondered: Was he with another woman when he could be home teaching me to take a picture/drive a stick shift/make potato pancakes?

"In the fall of 1991, I flew back to boarding school in California from our home in New York; my father had driven me to the airport. Once at my dorm, I called home, and my mother sounded strange on the phone: "Your father never came home." He'd hugged me at the United terminal, then gotten in his car and driven all the way to Arizona, to his mistress. I remember thinking, How could he not tell me he wasn't coming back?

"But then he did come back. A few months later, he showed up at my graduation—tan, fit, wearing a linen suit, his white hair longer than I'd ever seen it. I never spoke to him about his family sabbatical.

"My father died 10 years ago and, to be fair, he was a great deal more than his infidelities. He had a Dickensian childhood—raised in an orphanage, knew only poverty, never dreamed of going to college. He was highly intelligent (he invented film-processing systems that revolutionized photography), generous and so handsome that Catherine Deneuve flirted with him and Audrey Hepburn tried to buy him a drink. (He declined. I never learned why.) I take after my father in many ways—I got his dark eyes, his hot temper, his taste for burned toast. And I understand why he cheated: There wasn't enough love in the world to make up for what he'd missed as a child. I just wish I wasn't doomed to repeat it."

Danielle Pergament has plenty of company. A girl abandoned by her father will often live her life unconsciously seeking to fill her craving for the affection she didn't get and that bored a hole into her heart. The world is full of women, and men, who try to fill this emptiness with diversions and addictions—fantasy relationships, drugs, food, shopping, alcohol, and fame among them. They pour these short-term pleasures into the top of their hearts, only to see them flow right back out through the hole at the bottom. This emotional cotton candy looks enticing, tastes sweet, and doesn't last.

That pursuit of fool's gold can last a lifetime for those who don't awaken to its insatiable nature. When that hole gets seared into a daughter's heart, it's burned from the inside; it gets healed from the inside, too, not from some elixir "out there." And that healing is hard work. I know that from my own experience.

Even more difficult for a daughter is the healing from physical, emotional, or sexual abuse. Cultures around the world punish their most heinous crimes with imprisonment or death. Abusive fathers dole out sentences of psychological imprisonment and emotional death to their daughters, not for guilt but for their innocence and powerlessness.

This ultimate betrayal by a father is a horror beyond comparison. And it's all too common. One in four US girls is sexually abused by the age of eighteen, and 30 to 40 percent of the cases involve family members.[2] You can add to that figure the girls who aren't sexually mistreated but who are physically or emotionally ravaged. An abusive relationship with one's father is a birthplace of hell on earth.

I heard heartbreaking stories of abandonment and abuse during my conversations. Here are accounts from women with the courage to share the lifelong pain conceived in their fathers' transgressions. Few women find the path to healing on their own. Rather, those I came to know found it through therapy, spirituality, and often surrogate fathers. And as Katie's story in particular shows, the human spirit has an enduring capacity for triumph.

---

2 There is a vast literature on this subject. See, for example:

Abel, G. & Harlow, N. (2001). Stop Child Molestation

Kilpatrick, D., Saunders, B., & Smith, D. (2003). Youth victimization: Prevalence and implications. US Department of Justice, National Institute of Justice report.

Snyder, H N. (2000). Sexual assault of young children as reported to law enforcement: Victim, incident, and offender characteristics. National Center for Juvenile Justice, US Department of Justice.

http://www.cdc.gov/nccdphp/ace/prevalence.htm

ACE Study - Prevalence - Adverse Childhood Experiences

A Touching Job

Luna was born in Ogden, Utah. She began using LSD, cocaine, and heroin in her mid-teens. At eighteen, she started supporting herself and her drug habit by selling her services as a sex worker.

When we met, she was a 32-year-old single mother of a young daughter and was putting herself through college by working as a sensual masseuse.

"Back in the day, I wasn't doing very good. When I was younger, I partied and got involved with drugs and just went to a really dark place. I started drinking and smoking pot and smoking when I was fourteen. I think I started doing acid and cocaine by the time I was fifteen or sixteen. By the time I was a junior in high school, things got really bad, because me and my friends got into amphetamines. I used to be a really bad heroin and coke addict. I was in and out of rehab and the last time I was there, I got kicked out.

"I definitely had a hard upbringing. I started doing the work that I do when I was eighteen. Later I had sex with men for more cash, so I could support my habit. It got really bad, even to the point that I was sleeping with dealers to get stuff. That was probably the biggest low that I hit.

"Now I basically do a full body sensual massage. I feel like my job is important and it's not just like perverts and this and that. I think that people overlook it or maybe look at it in a negative light, when it actually is something that's positive in some ways. What I've learned through my job is touch is an important thing that we overlook a lot of times. We really need to feel affection and touch from a person.

"I just think some people go so long without it and it's very healing, and it's very powerful just to have your hands on somebody else or be on the receiving end of that. I see all sorts of different people, from young to old to all shapes and sizes. Sometimes I'll see people that are handicapped or have limbs missing, people that are going through divorces or even married people."

I was struck by Luna's saying that, "It's very powerful just to have your hands on somebody else." I asked her if she found it healing to touch her clients. "I think it's a mutual thing. I think it's healing for me and the person. I haven't figured it all out for myself. I'm sure there are reasons that I'm not aware of why I've ended up doing the work that I do. I've just been doing this for so long. I'm probably going to end up crying."

And she did. I had known this woman, and she had known me, all of fifteen minutes. And now she was in tears.

I was touched by the tenderness and vulnerability of the many women like Luna who exposed so much of themselves in our conversations. The memories and feelings that came up while we were together were so raw, and often had been held inside for years. Every time I sat with women like Luna, and heard their stories of heartbreak, I could feel some of the pain they were sharing. I would simply sit with them and listen, let them express their hurt for as long as they needed, and talk about it with them as openly and authentically as I could. I never found this uncomfortable. I knew it would run its course. It always did.

When Luna regained her composure, she talked about her desire to have a stable relationship with someone she loves and who loves her. That desire, and wanting to provide better for her daughter, were driving her toward a college degree she'd just begun working on. She told me she enjoys helping people, and that she wants to work as a nutritionist. For now, she needs a well-paying job. With her education and skills, there aren't many options that pay as much as her erotic work, so she carries on.

Luna's eyes were red from crying, and her face was covered with mascara and dried tears. "Well," she said as we resumed the interview, "I knew that there was a good possibility of having emotions and wondered am I ready to cry in front of a stranger right now.

"I really don't have a problem with my job," she continued. "It's like any job. There are things about it that I like. There are parts about it that I don't like sometimes. I feel like it might be kind of an addiction for me in a weird way, too. Or it's just like a comfort zone. It's all I've known for so long now, I could probably just do it forever. But it's not something that I want to do forever and there's a lot of reasons why I want to do something different. But I've put it off for so long, just because I'm comfortable doing it and I make really good money. I'm able to take care of myself plus my daughter."

Luna talked openly about the neglect, abandonment, and abuse she grew up with.

"My mom had me when she was fifteen. My dad was four years older than my mom. He was really never a part of my life growing up. I thought my sister's dad was my dad until I was like eight years old and then my mom told me. I remember my mom saying, 'You know, it's not like I'm keeping you from him. He knows about you. He's just too busy doing his thing or partying.'"

The man Luna assumed to be her dad—her sister's father—didn't stay around long, leaving when she was four or five. Soon after that, Luna had her third father figure. "My mom had boyfriends and she met my step-dad when I was eight, and they married when I was ten. They've been together off and on since then.

"And so, back to my dad, I met him when I was nine. I remember coming home and my mom was like, 'Oh, this is your dad.' And I was like, 'Hi…' I just felt weird. I didn't really know how to be. I was like, 'You're my dad I've been wanting to see?' I just didn't know what to say. 'Oh, where have you been all my life?' I was just young and I was like, 'Wow, okay, this is a little awkward.' I guess I was just kind of in shock. But, I was kind of in a weird way excited. I was like, 'Oh, well, I have a whole other thing out there that I don't really know anything about.'"

After the shock and some excitement wore off, Luna said she was filled next with curiosity about her father and the family she'd not known. Luna's mother and father ran into each other occasionally after that, and "she'd bring him home and they'd hang out and party together and then he'd be gone and I wouldn't see him. And then, probably like a year and a half later, she brought him home again."

It took several more years before Luna got to know the blood family she had on her father's side. "Once my cousin's dad and my grandma invited me to this family reunion and I met an entire family that I'd never met before. My dad was actually in jail at the time, but I met all these people. I got to talking with my cousin. I told him I had went to rehab for heroin, and it just so happened that him and his friends started using it. So it was like bad timing, because I felt really connected with him at first. I was going to parties where he would DJ, and I met all his friends, and we started using together. He actually overdosed in my apartment once and almost died.

"My family found out about it and they were mad at both of us. And that was when I started talking to my dad. He started calling me from jail. 'I know I haven't been there your whole life. I heard about what happened.' He wasn't judgmental. He was just like, 'You don't want to end up where I am.' And so we started to establish a relationship. So when I'd go back to Utah, I'd go hang out with him after he got out of jail."

I wondered if Luna even had a man whom she identified as a father. She didn't. "I don't feel like I could say that any of them were really my father, to be honest. Even my own dad. He's my father by blood. I accept that and I care about him. But he's got six kids with five different women. My dad's never really been there. He's an addict. He never put a lot of effort forth. When I finally started to get to know him he was doing better. He was sober for a while. But he's just my father because of blood.

"My sister's dad, things are just fuzzy. He did play a role in my life when I was younger and I thought he was my dad. I don't have anything negative to say. He's cool when I see him, but he's just kind of a weird guy. And then there's my step-dad, who was present in my life as a father more than any of these guys. But I don't like to accept him as my father. I have a lot of anger towards him. He's just done a lot of really messed-up things to me and my mom, my family.

"My step-dad was very abusive to my mom. When I was younger I would sneak out of the house in the middle of the night to call the police, because he was beating my mom up. And there were a few times where he got physical with me, and he was verbally abusive. He's just a jerk.

"Mostly it was with my mom, but, yeah, there were times where he choked me, threw me down on the ground, took my head and slammed me into a corner. I always ended up being the one getting punished about it, because then when I did something about it and tried to let authorities know, I ended up in this group home, all because he beat me up. So I got out of my house as soon as I could. He was never sexually abusive. Thank God for that. That would really suck.

"He had a hard upbringing and he's just really ignorant, too. He'd say things to us like, 'If you ever bring a nigger or a spic home, I'll kick your ass.' That kind of stuff. He just thinks he knows it all about everything."

I asked Luna if she had a sense of how she was shaped by not having a close father or one with permanence.

"I don't really know," she replied. "I'm sure maybe it has something to do with my choices sometimes in men that I'm attracted to. Sometimes I've reflected after I've had an experience with a guy that didn't go so great, if that had anything to do with it—just maybe I've dated a few guys that ended up just being jerks.

"But my mom and my stepdad, their relationship is crazy. And that's what I saw growing up. It's just like my mom could never break free from a bad situation. My mom's a really bad alcoholic, and my step-dad is more of a functioning one, because he works. So he can do his business, but my mom hasn't had a job in probably six or seven years. She would wake up and start drinking. It was just crazy growing up. I never knew what was going to happen. It was like walking around on eggshells. Sometimes I'd come home and they'd be drunk already. You never knew when they were going to get in a fight or what was going to happen."

Luna had broken attachments to each of her three father figures. I asked if she saw how that affected her ability to function in relationships with men. "Yeah," she said, "that among other things, like just my job. I haven't had a lot of serious relationships like some other people have. And the few times that I did have long-term relationships, there are all sorts of issues, but one of them was I felt like sometimes I would almost create a problem because I didn't feel deserving or just like you said, that things might not last.

"And I don't think I really noticed that right away, but then I started thinking about it at one point and figured that probably did have something to do with it, because I'm not used to things going so smooth. I think I have some definite issues. I guess it's hard for me to really know the full meaning of what it's like to be really connected with somebody like that. And since I don't really know, I don't really have anything to compare to.

"I hope to have it come to light for me a little bit more clear. It's affected what kind of guys I choose, and sometimes it's not even conscious. I have such a wide variety of types of guys that I'm attracted to. I've picked guys that were just kind of jerks and I've put up with their crap. And then I kind of look back and I'm like, 'Why would I do this?' And then if I really think about it, think back about how I felt about my mom, like why did my mom put up with my step-dad's crap?

"So, I haven't had a lot of serious relationships, because when my friends were getting that experience, I was a drug addict. Drugs were my relationship in the early days. I don't think I've ever been in a relationship longer than two years.

"That's another thing that's hard about my job—it makes it hard for me to find a partner. And I don't like to lie. So if I ever find somebody, I'm going to either have to be out of this work or it's going to have to be somebody who is secure, strong enough in their own self. If I met somebody, I'd be willing to stop what I'm doing to be with them, because if I loved somebody I would trade whatever.

"There have been a couple times where I've met guys and I started to care for them a lot and the job was interfering and I was willing to make that step. But in order to make that step, I also wanted some commitment. I wanted to know, 'You're going to be there for me, because this isn't easy. I've been doing this like my whole life.' So the guy I meet is going to have to be patient and willing to work with me and be understanding that it'll be a little bit of a process transitioning out.

"That's why I'm going to school now, too. I just feel like my work keeps me from having the connections that I could want to have. That's probably the most painful part of what I do. I've gotten used to making a certain amount, so I've got payments that match up to that amount. I know I can do anything I set my mind to. I just know it's not going to be easy and it sure would be nice to have a little help.

"It's scary. It's going to be a while before I graduate from school. I haven't done anything for so long. I don't have a resume. I don't really know how I'm going to do things. I'm just winging it. I don't have a clear path ahead of me. I'm just kind of like, 'Okay, I'm doing something. At least it's something.' Because I don't have anything else to fall back on."

Luna had spoken earlier about how her hands-on work can be healing for her as well as the men she's with. So I asked her if any of those relationships ever touched her at a deeper level. What she told me didn't seem that surprising.

"I wouldn't say fully, but sometimes, yeah, depending on the person. Sometimes you just have a connection with somebody, no matter what. I've taken chances and I've explored some connections with two people that I've met. There have been a couple different men that I've met over the years that I've become really close friends with, where I even stopped seeing them for anything work-related, because we became friends and I talked to them all the time.

"And what's really kind of strange is I've had a couple of them step in and kind of play a fatherly role in my life. There's this one guy that I met years and years ago. I saw him for years. He was my regular client. And then I started going out to lunch with him when he came into town. And then he told me, 'We've become such good friends, I just can't really, like, see you like that anymore. It doesn't feel right.'

"I just felt very comfortable with him, I could talk to him and he listened. And he's done a lot of things for me, he co-signed on a car for me, he co-signed on apartments for me, he's lent me money. He's given me trust that I don't really have with my family.

"I had another guy who told me that he was a painter and that he was looking to paint a different subject and he wanted to chat with me and he also said that he was a dentist, as well. What rang the bell for me that time was like, 'Yes, I need dental work.' So I ended up meeting with him. He never painted me, but we became friends. He's an older married guy. And he's just kind of lonely even though he's married. He and his wife don't even sleep in the same room any more. And we just enjoyed each other's company because he's just really sweet and I got free dental work.

"There's an older gentleman, too, that I met over the summer. And he's retired and just such an interesting character. I saw him originally as a session. But he's so old, nothing really happens there. His whole kick, he would just go around and meet all of these escort girls. I think he just has a lot of money and curiosity. He's got to be eighty-something. The first time I came to see him, he was just really sweet. He brought me flowers. And then he ended up calling me back more. His wife had passed away four or five years ago. And I could tell that he's lonely.

"He's gifted me with so many things. I never asked for them. And I felt uncomfortable about it, like, he's being so nice to me. I feel like I'm taking advantage. It's like too nice. He bought me an iPhone. He bought me iPhone players, dinners, jewelry, a crock-pot."

I told Luna I thought he probably wanted someone to open his heart to, and that he probably feels affection for her.

"I know now," she replied. "I talked to him about it, because I told him that I felt like that and he reassured me. He's like, 'I want to do this. You're not making me do this. I'm older, I have some extra money to spend, so don't feel like that.'

"So even though I didn't have a dad, I'm finding my dad in lots of people."

During the hours that Luna and I spent together, I saw the biological father who was too busy partying to help raise her, the surrogate father who left before she was five, and the stepfather who was an ignorant brute. They were in the red eyes and the dried tears and makeup on her face.

How, I wondered, do fathers simply throw away their daughters? I wonder what would happen if every father could sit with women, as I did, and listen to the pain inside women who have been abandoned or abused. I can't help but think they'd find it a lot harder to discard their daughters so carelessly.

These women, by the way, are all around us. They're journalists, teachers, co-workers, bosses, soccer moms. Like all of us, they put on their masks of composure and go out into the world and, hiding their painful inner life, do the best that they can.

The Wrong End of a Gun

Courtney and I met at the orientation for our junior high school during our last month of elementary school. I ended up standing in a line next to her, and we talked about who was going to be the toughest kid in seventh grade when all the schools came together.

I thought it was a kid named Pee Wee from my elementary school. She thought it was a guy named Paul from hers. Actually, it may have been Courtney. There probably weren't any others like her who, in the coming year, would pull a gun and point it at their fathers, and then in a life-defining moment face the decision of whether to pull the trigger.

An only child, she's been married once, and it was brief. She's held a number of jobs, but for the last several years she's not been working. She lives with her elderly mother, who is in frail health.

In her interview, Courtney usually referred to her father as "he" or by his name (Ron), reflecting her emotional distance from him.

Ron was born in Mississippi in 1934, the son of a sharecropper. "They were dirt poor," Courtney told me. "Five kids and they lived in a one-room shack. He worked in the cotton fields. I don't believe he got more than an eighth grade education. His father died when he was eleven or twelve, from a penicillin shot. Everybody saw him die.

183

His mother was a mean-ass bitch—an angry, bitter, hateful woman. His dad worked hard Monday through Friday, but he would take off on the weekend and go get drunk. He was a no-good son of a bitch until the day he died.

"When his dad died, his mother married an awful man, but he had a general store and he had money. At fifteen or sixteen, Dad got into the Air Force to get out of Mississippi and away from a really shitty life. He found himself in Korea. For a fifteen or sixteen year old, Korea and the military were not good. There were lots of hookers. When I was a kid I saw some pictures of what was going on that kind of warped him sexually. They shouldn't have been where I could get hold of them.

"He met my mom, Norine, in Kansas. He was an alcoholic, but stopped drinking when he was in a horrible accident and got his butt thrown in the brig. I would call him a dry drunk right now.

"He was discharged from the Air Force in 1953. I think he was out here for a year and then went back and married Mom in 1955. I was told I was an accident, that I was the hole in the diaphragm. Mom's eight years older than Dad, and he was still a kid. I don't think they knew what they were getting into. And they were in over their heads. But they bought a house and moved out to the 'burbs. It's the house I'm still in.

"I was born in '57. We didn't spend much time around his family. The first time I remember going to Mississippi, I was seven. And of course that was during the civil rights movement and I was going to school when two young men were murdered. My dad's sister was married to a Klansmen. I don't have a lot of use for the South.

"I don't have a lot of early family memories. I don't know if that's by choice or what. I think when I was born he was a baker. You hear of people talking about memories from when they were three and four years old—not me. A neighbor, Bernie, used to take care of me. And I have a lot of memories of being around her kids and all the kids she took care of. That was probably where I was the happiest.

And then I would go home and deal with two people who were very angry at each other. I look at family pictures and I don't see anybody who looks happy. He told me a year before I got married he never wanted to marry Mom, but she was pregnant.

"I don't remember home being a happy place. I tried to stay away as much as I could as I got older, to play with the kids in the neighborhood and just be out and going and going and going. Mom was not a loving person. He was not a loving person. He was an angry man; he yelled and screamed a lot and she was submissive and then when he would leave, I would get her toxic crap. I have some memories of being home with her and just being by myself a lot. I was really good at playing by myself. I didn't have any warm fuzzy feelings. None.

"I can't tell you a birthday where I was ecstatic. I remember one Christmas that was different because my cousin and his wife came up from San Diego. It was just nice because it wasn't just the three of us. The last five years he couldn't wait to get out of the house to get to whoever he was having an affair with—and it was always a sigh of relief for me when he was out. The last few years he'd always make an excuse to go someplace.

"There was not a great quality of relationship with either one of them. He would come home and mow the yard and expect dinner on the table and he was always doing something outside the house. Or he was glued in front of the TV. Neither one of them knew how to make a cohesive family. I never saw them hug, never saw them kiss. I just always felt this tension. She was angry that he left his good union job as a baker and got into this grocery store. I just remember a lot of anger."

Courtney said her father was verbally abusive, and began sexually abusing her when she was five or six.

"He molested me, and I am 99.9% sure I was raped. I was twelve or thirteen. Mom was out of town on business. She should have come home that night, but she decided not to, and I paid a price for that. I remember certain things. I'll be going along doing something, at home or asleep, and something will lift me up and I'll go, 'Oh, holy crap.' It's like a veil came down and I don't remember it. One of my best friends from back then remembers when my personality changed and the anger came out."

Shortly after that, Courtney had her hand on the trigger of a gun aimed squarely at her father. "He had my dog outside, beating the hell out of it with a dictionary. I grabbed his German Luger in one hand, and I had the clips in the other. He's scared shitless of guns. He was robbed twice when they had the grocery stores, and he was kidnapped the second time.

"And he got away from the dog, and started crawling on all fours away from me. I told him I'd kill him, and I meant it. I meant it. And it wouldn't have taken much. The only thing that kept going off in my head was, 'If you kill him, you're gonna have consequences.' It was like God was a woman screaming really loud, 'Don't do it; he isn't worth it.' It was a weird thing. I couldn't stand up for myself but I could for my dog. So he left me alone after that. I've never picked up another gun in my life."

At that point, Courtney broke down and cried. I was seething with anger as I sat with her. I wanted to kill the bastard. This was a woman I'd grown up with. I recall asking myself, "How in the name of God does somebody recover from that?" Perhaps that recovery started when she found the courage to pull the gun.

"On one hand," she said of nearly shooting her father, "it was terrifying. And on another it was quite liberating. I got control back on some level. It felt really good. I probably also could have kicked the crap out of him. He wasn't that big. And the funny thing is, Mom was home, and she remembers none of it. That's their warped way of dealing with it. Nothing ever happened. I separated it from the rest of my life. What gave me stability was my caretaker family, not my birth family. I could go down there and be around them and I was like the little sister.

"I did tell Mom that I wanted to be adopted, I didn't want to live there anymore. I was in junior high. I cried all the time. My personality was very different at home. I was not allowed to be funny, to be any of those things. I had to clean the house, I had to have chores, I had to do things, I had to keep them...I think my job was to keep them together on some bizarre level. And for what reason, I don't know.

"He was always screwing around on Mom, and we always knew that. She always made me a part of that, whenever he was having an affair. I had to intercept the phone calls and the mail. This woman would call the house and she would yell at me and tell me, 'The only reason your dad's staying is because of you, blah blah blah.' And I was like, 'Hmmph, don't stay because of me. I can't stand the bastard.' I was probably in fourth, fifth, sixth grade. There was so much dysfunction and stupidity going on.

"He left for good when I was fifteen. Praise Jesus; he was gone. I didn't miss him. Then I had to deal with her, curled up in a ball. She had a nervous breakdown, and I took care of stuff. She literally just checked out. I would make the grocery list and tell her what she had to do, and I paid the bills. My friends from high school said that I was the adult, parenting her."

I asked Courtney if she was aware of what she came to believe about herself, growing up with an angry, distant, and abusive father, and in a family filled with tension.

"I took a lot of the brunt of it. I was called an idiot, stupid, a conceited bitch. I think for a lot of years I believed it. And I was probably in my twenties when I figured out I wasn't stupid. And that those statements were probably as much about himself.

"This whole parenting thing was not something they ever should have done under any circumstances. And that's why I didn't want kids. I knew at twelve or thirteen that I didn't want to put anyone through what I'd gone through. And until I got a divorce and started dealing with a lot of crap, I didn't realize I'd made an adult decision at a young age. I knew I didn't have any motherly instincts. Some people think, 'Oh, you missed the boat, oh, you should have.' And no, I shouldn't have. I had nothing to give.

"There just comes a point in time where you go, 'I don't want to remember this garbage.' You bury it deep, really deep. And as an adult, those things do come back. But it's whenever you're more solid as a person, or in a better environment. And things will pop up. Once in a while I'll go, 'Whoa, where did that come from?'

"I made the decision two or three years ago that I did not want him in my life. I was done. He got back into my life because for eight years I had nothing to do with him after my divorce, and I had to deal with all of the abuse from him. I put myself in therapy and dealt with it. He wormed his way back in 1991 and '92, showed up on the doorstep crying and I let him in. I was very guarded. And then two or three years ago he lit into me when I was taking care of Mom. He called me every name in the book, and I just said, 'That's it. I have boundaries, you've crossed every one of them, I'm done.'

"I feel a lot of relief that that person will not come back into my life. I don't care if his wife drops dead and the state calls me. I'm not taking care of him. He doesn't have a clue as to how to be a kind, caring, loving person. He didn't have it in his life, and he doesn't know how to give it.

"I think the kindest thing my dad ever did for me, and he did it for himself, on my fifth birthday we picked out the dog. But it was really that my dad wanted a dog. I got a water ski one year for my birthday. Well, it was the water ski he wanted."

Courtney and I talked about her father's attitudes toward women, and how women were worthless in his eyes. Between that and the abuse she suffered, I wanted to know how she thought that shaped her self esteem and relationships with men.

"I don't think I've ever felt worthless. I've had times where I've thought, 'You know, if I'd been raised in a better environment, I wouldn't have made that choice.' I haven't fought as hard for myself as I probably should have. I think for me, and this is a flip, but I've always tried to make my mother love me. I don't know if that comes from feeling worthless or not getting what I should have gotten from her.

"How did I feel about myself—today I still struggle with it. I've avoided relationships for ten or fifteen years and decided I'd concentrate on my career. That wasn't a smart thing to do, but I did it. You know, it was easier. It's understandable, I'm sure there were some nice guys that I just blew off and said, 'Right now I'm busy. I'm working too many hours. I don't have time to date.' I was really good at that.

"The thing I've learned about a lot of women who have been molested and raped, most of them go off on a tangent and start having sexual relations really young. I went in the opposite direction screaming, 'Get your lips off me or I might twist them off!'

"There were guys that I happened to be involved with as I got older that weren't the right people for me. They didn't have a healthy sense of their sexuality, either. My ex-husband certainly didn't. I don't like to talk about this one, but I had an affair with someone who was married. That was in my early thirties. But after that, I really kind of stood back and went, 'What is it that I really want?' And that's when I put all of my energy into work.

"I'm very straight up with guys. I don't talk about feelings! Nope, I just get to the point, 'Let's get it done, what do we need?' I don't know, that probably filled up a part of me that I'd never felt before, being successful and knowing what I was doing and I was good at."

Another step in Courtney's recovery was beginning therapy during her divorce, when she was about 27, she recalled. "I was still married when I first went into therapy and I went for seven or eight years on and off. I didn't go back into it until about ten years ago. I had issues around, 'Where was Mom during these years?' I worked with the therapist for a few years on that, and then he died.

"He was a much older man and he was just really good. He was kind of like the solid dad you didn't get. He reminded me of Santa

Claus. A very nice, stable guy. I got a different perspective from him than you get from women. It was really good. I haven't found anyone since. I haven't really looked. I've had other issues to deal with."

Growing up with that kind of vulnerability, I wondered if Courtney had internalized beliefs around the world being a dangerous place.

"Only with them," she said. "I remember my caretaker Bernie taking me to the bus stop. I had a little note pinned on me. And it said where I was to get off, and I would get on the bus and go downtown and meet my mom. I was five, six, seven. I was told to sit by the bus driver. I always looked at it with a sense of adventure. I didn't feel scared. I think traveling as a little girl, being pulled out of your classroom and being put in a strange environment in Kansas, and then to be also in the middle of Mississippi during the civil rights movement helped me not fear the world. Life's an adventure.

"But my sense of who I am and what I've done, it didn't come from them. It really came from Bernie. And the older I've become the more I realized that. Her job was to take care of me and she did. There's a concept! I was really fortunate in that respect. I didn't realize it until after she died in 1991. And it was too late to thank her. She was a rock."

I asked Courtney what else, if anything, she felt like she absorbed from her father and their relationship. She wasn't sure.

"Obviously I've taken something from him, but what it is, for good, bad or indifferent, I don't know if I've thought very hard about it. He had a public persona of being friendly, happy-go-lucky and I think I mirrored that. I've met people along the way, teachers, people I've worked with that I've respected, that I've gotten more from than I've ever gotten from those two. Maybe when they're dead I might ask, 'What did I get from them?'

"I was competitive. I used to just love to ski my old man into the ground. I was better at waterskiing than he was. And that's not something a lot of girls do. But it was my way of giving him the big finger.

He got angry about that. Not in a way that you would notice it, but he did things and took chances in the boat with me on the back of it that he should not have done.

"I got hurt once because of his stupidity. I had a really long line, and when you have a really long line and you do a really tight hairpin turn, the whip is really strong—and there was a big wake and he knew it. I was stretched out and I went down with my arm up and I was hurt. He never apologized.

"He was at my wedding. He had told me that he would not walk me down the aisle. He thought Mom was gonna arrest him. Yeah. So I asked his brother. And then Bernie got on the phone and said to Ron, "What the hell? She doesn't ask anything of you.""

Driving Off
the Cliff

I have an unconventional past mixed with my somewhat conventional career. I've lived in some of the great countercultural centers of America: Berkeley, Santa Cruz, and San Francisco, California; Portland, Oregon. I was a drummer. I have friends who I swear live on other planets. For a guy, I can get pretty far out there. But I never, *never* took astrology seriously.

About ten years ago my wife gave me a birthday gift of a session with an astrologer named Carol Ferris. When I walked out of Carol's office after two hours with her, my head was spinning. She didn't know me until we met. And then she told me my life story. She was so exacting in comprehending my inner conflicts and turmoil. I found our time together enormously helpful. And I never forgot Carol.

When I was recruiting women to interview, I reached out to her. I wanted to know more about this woman and what role her father played in her life. I looked forward to trading places with her, and listening to her story, not mine. She was 65 at the time of our interview.

Carol's father Benson was born May 5th, 1922 in Moscow, Idaho, the son of a lumber baron who built and ran huge sawmills on the Clearwater and Snake Rivers nearby. Carol described her grandfather as "an original and a man's man, a hard drinker, a hard worker, a smart manufacturing guy, a smart woods guy and really comfortable in the out of doors." One thing he didn't do, she said, was spend a lot of time with his family.

Her father inherited many of those traits. "My dad was the oldest son and the star of the family. He had a sister who was two years younger and a brother who was eight years younger. He was a star athlete, incredibly gifted physically, really handsome, and kind of a stud. He inherited the love of drinking and hanging out and having a good time.

"Because they were small-town wealthy in the lumber business in the twenties, thirties, and forties, he had a really nice life. He went to the University of Idaho, where he met my mom. They married in 1942 when he went into the Navy in World War II, serving as an aircraft pilot in the Pacific. Then they went to Florida, where he did his basic training.

"He really loved flying, he loved the adrenaline. Like a lot of people who are martial in their natures, the chaos and energy of competition and those situations suited him. I don't think life was ever as interesting for him after the war, after being young and kind of on top of the heap.

"Dad was the manager of a semi-pro baseball team, and he was the pro at the Lewiston Golf and Country Club. He was trying to make a living doing what he loved to do, being an athlete and hanging out and drinking and teaching people how to play golf and baseball. His parents were supplementing his income and we only lived a mile away from them."

In Carol's seventh and eighth year, her sister and youngest brother were born. Her father gave up the livelihood he loved to earn more money to support his family. From the fraternity of sports he moved to working as an appliance salesman in Utah. He hadn't completely given up on his carefree life, it turned out. "He was drinking pretty hard and we later found out he had been having a lot of sex outside the marriage all of those years. The marriage was pretty shaky and he wasn't happy being a salesman in Utah."

Soon after, the family moved to Eugene, Oregon. "That's when my parents' marriage really fell apart," Carol said. "Dad was hired by Payless to be the manager of their appliance department, and Mom and Dad separated. The separation and divorce were very, very difficult for everybody."

Benson moved in with his lover and started to work his way up the company management chain, moving around the Pacific Northwest. "He saw very little of his children all those years. They moved to Florida when he was in his sixties. They moved back eventually, because he was diagnosed with cancer."

Carol's father was at war during the first few years of her life, a critical period during which the imprint is laid down in a child's developing mind about trust and intimacy. Carol saw that broken attachment with her father play out in her life. "I would say it characterized everything.

"In astrology and in Jungian psychology, the archetype of father is a pulse, an archetypal being at work in the cosmos, with a particular shape in all human life. In Chinese philosophical thinking, the function of fatherness is to create structures that define and hold and contain meaning. No father means no structure and no meaning.

"So, not only was my dad not physically present in those first two years, but he never really wanted to be a father. It just happened because he liked to fuck. In terms of creating structure and meaning in the lives of his family, he did not see that as his job. He wasn't able to do it. In retrospect, of course, his own model of fatherness was that his dad got up and went to work and came home and drank scotch and partied and went to bed. I think part of it is the kind of modeling that he had about the responsibilities of a father.

"As a part of my own therapeutic process, I had to go back and think about all the things in my childhood, all these father-daughter things like Blue Birds and PTA and things at school, and Dad was just never there. He had no interest in our lives, in who we were as people.

"I said to my husband, 'Don't you get it why I'm married to someone my dad's age, and that the people that have played the biggest role in my life have been older men who've been mentors?' I kept looking until I found someone that would see who I was and help me make decisions that would give meaning to my life." Carol said she finally found those men, but not without flailing somewhat aimlessly.

"When I was in college, I was drinking and smoking dope and screwing around. I got pregnant and had an abortion. Then, I got pregnant again and decided, 'Okay, time to get real.' After dropping out of the University of Oregon to have her son, she regrouped, returned to school, and completed a bachelor's degree in liberal arts.

"My family knew about the first pregnancy, the abortion, and at about that time, my dad's mother had a massive stroke. My dad said, 'Get over here and see your grandmother, because I think she's going to die,' and he was really freaked out. We had a really bad fight, actually a really great fight, where he talked about my life and that it was my fault she'd had a stroke, because I'd had this abortion and what kind of a girl was I?

"I remember saying to him, 'You have no idea what kind of a girl I am. You haven't been around.' And he just blew his stack. He picked me up and threw me against a wall. He pointed out the window of my grandmother's apartment and he said, 'Do you see that world out there? People get up every day. They go to work every day. They come home every day. They do the same things every day. Why can't you do that?' I said, 'Well, my life is not like that.'

"It was years later that I realized his own need to be free to do what he wanted to do, and the limitations that he'd agreed to in being a salesman, being married, having children that he didn't want to have, all of those things, that he never got to live the kind of life he wanted to live. And when he saw me making those choices, he didn't like it very much. But I didn't understand that at the time.

"My life wasn't that great, but it was mine. I have a very practical, conventional, down-to-earth nature and I also have a real wild streak. And so the apple didn't fall very fall from the tree. I just happened to have been born at a time when the culture made it possible for me to more fully live out those contradictions than his culture did. And I don't think he liked it very much. So I felt really sorry for him that he didn't get to live his life. He shouldn't have been a dad. He was not cut out for it. He barely could structure his own life."

As Carol spoke, her body and face began to sink with sadness. I asked her about that. "Yeah, it's sad.

"We were raised not to be angry. Don't set Dad off, be quiet, don't interfere. And so to actually have a fight with him, to say what was on my mind and to draw some boundaries and to begin to define myself in relationship to this sort of psychological amorphous mass who was very angry and really scared about his mom, with all this anger looking for somewhere to land—it couldn't go to his brother and sister and their spouses and so I was kind of the logical candidate.

"It was a really important moment for me, to resist having the guilt and shame and piss-offedness imposed on me, which he'd managed to lay off on the whole family for years. It's like his unhappiness was everybody else's fault."

Carol felt disliked by her father all of those years growing up, and carried feelings of guilt because of it.

To not feel loved or desired by her father, particularly an absent father, and not forming a bond during her first years, had to have consequences emotionally, and had to profoundly shape her sense of her desirability as a woman and her confidence in relationships with men. These are the unintentional lessons that no parent sets out to teach a child, yet they get laid down with enormous impact. Carol and I spoke about that next.

"I was really hurt and didn't know who I was. I didn't know what my talents were. I didn't know what I looked like. I didn't know how to dress. And I just was lost. I had got my feet under me as a mother and I was able to put a roof over our heads and work and nurture my son. But that was the only identity that I had to hang onto.

"And I couldn't say that I dated anybody; it was more like having occasional sexual relationships. I didn't feel attractive, I often felt invisible, didn't care about how I looked, tended to be involved in groups of people or in families who'd needed a chief cook and bottle washer and an organizer and a child care provider. So my dad wasn't there emotionally and psychologically and often physically, and my mom was what I now understand to be dissociated. We all knew how to do that, to pretend we were somewhere else, or to just be sort of an observer.

"Learning astrology showed me that there was an order in the world, that you could know it had a rhythm and a sense to it, and that people did have places in the world. And so the idea of a self that was a contained, supported, continuous, conscious, integrated self began to grow in me, starting about when my son was two or three years old.

"It wasn't conscious then, but I think Dad was very confused about women and his own sexuality. I think the whole family's very hot-blooded, very strong sex drives, but there was a really ambivalent relationship to that. And I was sort of part of that rebellion, that sex is okay. Except it wasn't very happy sex. I didn't know what I was doing and I didn't trust myself. I didn't know the meaning of my life. I was really lost.

"I was very surprised when somebody finally saw me. My husband really saw me. We got married three weeks after we met. He had been widowed for a year. I had just put my son on the plane for Georgetown. And we fell in love and got married. He sees me. That's been great.

"And I had a mentor in corporate life who saw me, and it really made a difference. And I've had two major teachers, one a painter and one a writer, they saw me. So all along the way, my own inner father got strong and sort of said, 'Well, let's find somebody who's really good at this.' It wasn't conscious at the time, but it happened."

The corporate mentor who "saw" Carol was an interesting surrogate father, and an intriguing father-daughter dance unfolded between them. A single mother at the time, Carol began her twenty-year corporate career in a lumber business as the sales vice president's secretary. Dissatisfied with the limitations of her role there, she left after nine months.

"So I'm at my new job, and the phone rings, and it's the secretary to the president and owner of that lumber company I had quit. And she said, 'I have to retire and I want you to take this job.' And I said, 'I don't want your job.' And she said, 'You meet me for lunch.' So we had lunch, and she said, 'This man is one of the smartest, most creative, most exciting, most dynamic, interesting, thoughtful, responsible human beings you will ever meet on the planet, and if you don't take this job, you're crazy. You come and interview him.' So, it was like, 'Oh, well, all right, I'll interview him.'

"He and I argued for an hour about why I didn't want to be a secretary and why I didn't want to work for a lumber business. And he said, 'I will call you Monday at your job at noon and you'll have your answer for me then.' That was Friday. So he calls Monday and says, 'You are coming to work for me, aren't you?' I said, 'Yes, I am.'

"After we'd worked together for two or three months, he said, 'Now that I see what you can do, we're going to get you into school; we're going to get you training; we're going to get you into management seminars. I can give you 25 to 30 percent of what I do, and that will free up my time to do what I do best for this company, which is to innovate and make it cook.' And that's what we did for years.

"Then I hit the ceiling and I said, 'Now what am I going to do?' And he said, 'I need for you to do what I need for you to do. I don't want you to do those other things.' So I found another job and left for two years. And one of the board members called and said, 'You need to go back. What do you want to do?' I said, 'I want to do public relations and lobbying and public policy and law.' And he said,

'Well, tell him that.'

"So we negotiated and I came back as a vice president. I was the first woman vice president in the company and one of the first woman vice presidents in the industry. He really saw me and we really loved each other. People thought we were having an affair, which was not true."

The father-daughter dance plays out in the workplace, with bosses and subordinates, and in women's choices of their partners. Here, Carol had an interesting story to share as well. A co-worker helped set in motion the events that led to Carol's marriage. The co-worker asked Carol why she wasn't married. Carol replied that she didn't know. Then the woman asked Carol if she had her "list."

"I said, 'My list? My list of what?' And she said, 'You know, your list of things you're looking for in a partner. You've got to have a list of ten things. Go home and write down a list of ten things. If I didn't have that list, I would never have married my husband.'

"So, I went home that night, had a couple of glasses of wine, got out a piece of paper and a pen, and I could only write down three things: Intelligent, Unconventional, Sexual. And I put my pen down and thought, 'Well, that explains a lot,' because that's the kind of guys I was attracted to.

"And then I picked up the pen again and I could not write. And I thought, 'Well, this is interesting. What can you not write?' And it was Faithful. I'd been with several intelligent, unconventional, sexual men who could not settle down. So I wrote the rest of the list, just writing stuff, not knowing really what I was writing. I kept my list in my recipe box, and when I cooked, I'd get it out and look at it.

"Over a period of about a year, I really worked on it. I began to realize that it wasn't a shopping list; it was a consciousness-raising exercise. There were things on the list that were true about me that maybe wouldn't be good in a relationship with another person.

"I didn't understand what some of those words meant in terms of a real person and the list started to look like a pretty interesting person, because who would be unconventional and conservative at the same time? What would that look like? And about three months later, I met Byron. And there he was. I completely believe that the radicalization of my consciousness transformed my nature and that when my nature transformed, it was visible to people who could see it."

I asked Carol if it was literally hard for her to write the word faithful. She said it was. And that it took her an hour to write it. "I didn't realize how important it was to me, because the family had fallen apart and I was carrying around a lot of guilt, the thing about, 'If we'd been better kids, would he have stayed?'

"I was remembering the incredible pain that the whole family went through because my dad was not faithful. And I was determined that I'm not going to do it if this isn't an ingredient in it. It was an incredible anchoring for me. I sort of built my persona on, 'It didn't matter to me.' Marriage didn't matter. Family didn't matter. None of that mattered. So to realize that it really mattered and that fidelity was a linchpin was a big breakthrough for me. It is the first conversation my husband and I had, about trust and fidelity.

"When that woman told me to write the list, I thought, 'This is the stupidest fucking thing I ever heard.' And the more I reflected on it, the more I saw that it was about giving a conscious shape to your life."

Carol was among the many women I interviewed who never heard her father say, "I love you." He came close to it on his death bed. "When he was dying, we four kids sat around his bedside. He was on heavy morphine when he was really close to the end, and he looked at me and said, 'Well, honey, I'm going to go all the way to the end and when I get there, I'm going to think about it and when I'm done thinking I'm going to come back and start over.' I think in this sort of morphine state, he really had some sense of the ongoingness of a spirit and that he was going to get a do-over. I said, 'Good, Dad, you do that.' He died about an hour later."

As she drove away that afternoon, Carol saw her father being loaded into a body bag. And she completely lost control of herself. "I could not drive, in the way that children cannot drive a car. I broke down and sobbed for quite a long time. I realized it wasn't just me, Carol, who would never have a chance to ever get it right with my dad, but it was the real deep sorrow of a child losing a parent. It was truly an archetypal experience, it wasn't personal at all.

"It was really sad. I had to just sit there until I could drive again. I felt like a seven or eight year old. And I thought about this dream I'd had when I was about seven, right after my sister was born. In the dream, we're all in the old '49 Chevy, except my sister. And my dad is driving fast and he's so angry. He drives straight up the bluff over the Snake River and turns the car around and he drives off the cliff, furious. And the car falls into the river, sinks in the river with this brown rushing water going by us.

"I think my dad was just crazy angry about his life."

What's Love Got To Do With It?

Deidra is of African ancestry, and moved to the US in her early twenties. At the time of our interview she was 48, and still competing internationally as a professional athlete. Because of her desire to remain anonymous, some details of her life, such as her sport, have been described only generally.

Deidra's father was born to a white mother and black father outside of the US. He grew up in a home with both parents, with whom he had a close relationship, though of the two his mother was the more distant and unaffectionate. "My grandmother was like my father," Deidra said, "not showing emotions, not showing love."

Deidra told me that her father had his first child when he was about twenty years old, before he was married. "Shortly after that he converted to Christianity and that's when he wanted to get married as soon as possible. He met my mother at 23, and got married at 24 or something like that.

"I think I was probably my father's favorite. I look like my father. When I was younger, everyone was skinny and I was the only one who had a little size. My father was not big but he was a tough-looking guy. I was always with my dad. So my mom would be upset sometimes because he would pay more attention to me than the other kids. And I think it was because I was tough, I could lift things,

203

I could throw things around. I was like one of his little sons, I think.

Deidra grew up on the farm her father owned, raising animals for food. He became a minister and then a bishop. "Every day our routine was get up at six, take care of the animals, come in, take a shower, go to school. After school, you come home at three o'clock, take care of the animals, take a shower and go to church. My father was a butcher, and on Saturdays we would have to get up early and prepare to kill sheep, pigs, cows, chickens, or whatever. And then we would kill the animals and he would go sell them."

Deidra has only a few memories of closeness with her father. "I can't remember my father even holding my hand. The only thing I can remember, I think I was probably four or five years old, one night my father pretended he was going in the van to get some ice cream or something. And he said, 'Oh, Deidra's sleeping, so let's leave her.' I remember I was so tiny, I was curled on my father's chest, pretending to be sleeping. So he took me and he put me in the chair and he said, 'Okay, let's go without her.'

"They turned the lights off in the house, while my mum hid behind the door and my father just crept outside with the others and turned the vehicle on, and when I heard that I just jumped up and I started to scream because I thought I was in the house by myself. That's the only thing I can remember where it was a kind of fun thing. I'll never forget that, because it's the only thing that happened where there was that closeness.

"And I can remember lying on my father's chest; I can never forget that. Other than that, there was nothing. There was no 'I love you.' Occasionally we would play dominoes. And I liked when we played dominoes because it made us feel close. But my father would be upset if he lost, so he couldn't lose! And those are the only couple things I can remember doing that gave me that kind of closeness to my dad.

"I think it all started to fall apart when I became eleven or twelve. That's the time when the relationship between my father and I dwindled, because my dad stopped sleeping in my mom's room. It just tore me apart because this is not what he preaches about, and I could see that they were drifting apart. I would stay up late at night in the living room and cry nonstop; uncontrollably. It felt as if my family was drifting apart.

"I know my dad really loved me a lot. And he came one night and he said, 'Okay, if I sleep in the room with your mum, would you stop crying?' And I said, 'Yes, I'll stop crying.' And he went and he slept in the room, maybe for one week. And after a week, it didn't work. I don't think my father ever loved my mother.

"Everyone thought we were the greatest family. He was the minister, he's a bishop. So he was not only a minister of that church, he was like an overseer of those churches. People looked up to him. People looked up to *us*. But no one knew what happened behind the walls. So there was this family that really wasn't a family, because my father was there but wasn't really there.

"My mum was really religious. And she always believed that God would change my father's heart and he would start sleeping in the same room again. He was the first thing in her mind and in her heart. She loved us, but she made sure that he got everything he wanted because that was her love. That was what she lived for, other than God."

Within a year, Deidra's father left the family, traveling to the US or England to work with churches. His attention to family responsibilities waned during Deidra's teen years, and by the time she was fifteen he had stopped supporting the family entirely. Even though she, her siblings, and her mother continued working the farm, her father would not allow them to take any of the animals for food. "He could be sweet, he could be nice, but that's it. He wouldn't ask, 'Are you okay? Do you have clothes, do you have money, do you have shoes?' He wouldn't ask anything, because he really didn't care."

Deidra came to the US on a student visa to attend college. One day when she was studying she received a call from her sister; their

60-year-old mother had just taken a serious fall and had an aneurysm. Deidra flew home, arriving on a Wednesday evening. Her mother died on Friday.

"I don't think I ever experienced hate and anger like I did until my mother passed away. And that hate and that anger was for my father. Although we worked so hard on the farm, my father would kill a cow or pig or sheep or chickens, and we would assist him, and he sold every single thing and never gave his family any.

"We had to help him run the farm, although he was not a part of the family anymore; and we did not share of the benefits of the farm. It still blows me away that my father could have been so insensitive and many times we may not have had our next meal and my father has a farm full of everything and he didn't care.

"My mum wanted so much to keep things under control and kept hoping that one day he would come home. She would leave all those goods and she would have to go to the supermarket to look for food for us. I am surprised that I don't hate my father when I think about that. I just don't understand it. I still don't know how anyone could do that, far less a minister. And it blows me away the kind of love my mother had until she died. That's a dangerous kind of love. It can kill you. You have to know when to walk away, and she didn't. She would just do everything to help him, do anything he wanted.

"You know, we loved her and she made us love our father. But it just came to a big head when my mother died and it felt as if the veil just moved away and we saw him as he really was.

"It was then that I felt such anger, so much anger, that I don't think I even grieved for my mother when she passed. When I returned to the USA I didn't really release and cry until about a year after my mother died. I think it was because of all of the anger and hatred that I felt. I don't think he ever knew how to be a father. I believe he loved us, but he never said, 'I love you.' He never said it to my mother. I never saw my father holding my mother's hand, I never heard him say, 'I love you,' I never heard him say, 'Thank you.'

I remember I really had to work on myself to get that anger out of me, because anger and hatred can be really destructive. It spills over into your life, into whatever you do.

"My father then was living in the United States and got married about a year after my mother died. That, too, was hard for us children to swallow. He asked to see us all. We met and he said, 'Well, I am going to get married to this lady. I've known her for 35 years. I asked her to get married before I asked your mother, but because she said no at that time, I decided to get married to your mother because I couldn't contain [remain celibate] as a young Christian.'

"I said to myself, 'If my father had the heart to tell his children that he didn't really love my mother, and he only got married because that's what the church wanted, I don't know what kind of heart he had.' I thought maybe over time my father would change and he would realize what he did. I don't think he has. I don't think he realizes what it really is to be a father or to love. He just gave up his responsibility of supporting his kids. Even if he didn't love my mother, if he had been there for us financially or there for us when we wanted anything, I think I would have had a lot more respect for my father. I love my father and whenever I go home I still look for him. But it's really hard to feel anything else, because that connection is not there.

"So there's nothing much that's good I can say about my father, and it's not because I hate him. It's because that's what's there, and that's what has been there for a long time.

"He lived in the United States for a while after he got married and I would go over to see him. I think that helped me in my healing process of getting rid of the hate and the anger. When I go home I go to see him, but I don't spend much time there. I normally see him for maybe ten or fifteen minutes, just go to make sure I say hello.

"So although my father still is a minister, I don't think he lived up to what he should have done, not only as a father, but as a minister who leads and instructs people to be better and to live better lives and have closer families. I think when my mother died, she died of a broken heart. I really believe that." Deidra began to cry.

"She believed in him. This is the thing that makes me cry. I don't know if he ever realized what the responsibility of a father should have been. I don't even think he does now. And he's not a crazy man. He's a smart businessman. I think he just cares about himself, and I don't know if he'll ever change. It's very difficult to even try to create a bond with my father even now, now he's almost 80 years old."

Our conversation moved to Deidra's sense of how her father shaped her.

"One good thing I think it did for my siblings and for me, too, it has caused us to love more, love our wives, husbands, partners, whatever. Love them more and be there for them because we know what we've been through and how we felt. We saw what our mother went through. I think that was more heartbreaking than anything, *anything*, because she loved my father to death, literally. So especially my brothers: they treat their wives so well, it's unbelievable.

"I have a sister who has been married twice, and another sister who's divorced, and I've never been married. I think the way our relationships are has a lot to do with how my father treated my mother. If we are not treated the way we should be treated, we don't let it slide. It has caused us to have high expectations for our husbands or our partners. We don't want to die of a broken heart. We don't want to love stupidly.

"We don't want to give our love away because I don't think that's love. As soon as love is not given back to you in return, it's not love anymore. And because of that, I think it has caused me to have very little tolerance for things that happen in my relationships."

I asked Deidra if that reciprocal nature of love doesn't also hold true with one's parents, and not just one's partner.

"When it's your father or your mother, you don't have a choice but to love them, if you want to continue to flourish, if you want to continue to grow, because you can't grow if you hate. You can't hate your father! You can't hate your mother. If they did the worst thing to you, even if you don't want to be a part of their life any more, you still love them because it's a part of you, it's a part of your blood. I look at myself sometimes and I see my father. I see my father because I'm a business woman. I'm aggressive where business is concerned. I'm a part of my mother: I love and care for my siblings, and I love deeply but not stupidly. So I'm my father and my mother. Because of that, it would almost be like hating a part of me if I hated my father.

"But because of what my father is even today, it has made it impossible for me to have that bond that I wish I could have, because that's not what he wants, and I wouldn't waste my time trying to get that from him because my mother tried forever, and we were there, and he never gave it to us either. I love him; I respect him as my father. But if I had an event to compete in on Saturday and my father died tomorrow, I would still go to compete."

I asked Deidra how she was able to release her anger, how she found the capacity to forgive, or if she simply acknowledged that she still feels anger toward him, yet loves him anyway.

"I think it was because of the way I grew up in the church. You love everyone. If you do something wrong, the first thing you have to do is go ask God to forgive you. The first time I felt hate for anyone in my life was for my father. I was 25 years old. It was terrible. I knew it just wasn't a part of me, it shouldn't be there, and that's when I asked to see my dad, and we talked about it, and it made me feel better just by letting it out.

"I called my father and it was a little before he got married, and we met in the park. For almost a year, I just was mad. I just hated him! I hated him, hated him. So we met and I talked about the whole thing and he actually said, 'Yeah, I wish I could have been there for you guys.' He was saying he was sorry that he wasn't there more for us, and then it made me feel better. Eventually I pretty much felt better and I got rid of the hate that I had for him, because that really helped me just release whatever it was inside of me.

"You would think that Christianity would take care of anything. It sounds bad to say, but I believe it made it worse. Or religion, I should say, made it worse. I think my father lived in religion but he was never Christ-like: loving his family, taking care of his family and having compassion. I never saw that. I just saw religion: 'You can't do *this*, you can't do *that*, you can't wear *this*, you can't wear *that*.' That's not what makes you. I think it breaks you. It breaks families up because you don't see the true value of people and it's hidden by all these formalities and that's all it is. That's sad, very, very sad, and the formalities become more important than who you're serving regardless of whether it's Christ or whatever else.

"My siblings and I, I think we're all spiritual, but we don't follow the religion any more that we grew up in. It really didn't help me. I think Christianity taught me how to forgive. Or it reminded me that I can't hate. I have to love. But I think it becomes dangerous when people allow the doctrine of whatever religion it is to overtake the good of whatever the real religion stands for. I think my father continues to allow it to sap the goodness out of his life by just focusing on the religion because that's important to him. I think he misses the boat by far and I don't think he realizes it."

I wondered how feeling that much anger toward her father, and how he abandoned his wife and children, shaped Deidra's beliefs about family life and men.

"I don't judge men based on my father. I still think that I judge people as individuals, regardless of if it's a man or a woman. Now because I'm gay, some people would say to me, 'Well, maybe it's because of how your father was to your mother.' I don't think that has anything to do with my father, because looking back on my life, I realize I have been attracted to the same sex maybe since I was five or six years old. I think if you have an attraction for the same sex, or whatever, it's been there forever.

"I know that I was probably fourteen years old when I really started thinking about it. I knew that I could never even talk to my father about that. I think my father would have beaten me to death. That was the intensity of religion in our family.

"Let me rephrase that. I think my father would have said to me, 'Never, ever let me hear you talk about that again.' He wouldn't have talked about it. If my father found me in a situation where I was involved in something like that, my father may have beaten me to death, I don't know.

"I never told anyone. I remember at lunch time I would go into this cathedral downtown and I would pray about it. I would say, 'You know, God, you're gonna have to help me with this because I don't know what this is. I don't know how to control it.' I would just pray about it, pray about it, to change it. As long as it was preached against, it was wrong. Until one day I came to a point where I said, 'You know, it's not religion that makes me who I am. It's my spirituality and it's what I want myself to become.'

"So I decided to put away religion. I decided to be done with that. When I put away religion, I felt like a bird. I felt like I took a really heavy armor off. I knew that religion was suppressing me into something that I was not; and unfortunately I think it happens to a lot of people who are really devoted to religion. I believe I am more spiritual now than I ever was."

I left my conversation with Deidra feeling a deep sense of sadness. She said several times during our interview that her father loved her. Perhaps he did. But love is selfless. He sounded profoundly self-centered. A father who loves his family does not leave them hungry, especially when they are working on his abundant farm.

I certainly know what it means to be self-absorbed. I had relationships in my early adulthood that I entered casually and left carelessly. Some of these were with extraordinary women. I wish I'd understood then what I know now. I would have been a very different partner.

My daughters re-created my understanding of love. That understanding—or more accurately misunderstanding—died when they were born. My heart exploded with unconditional love when each of my daughters came into the world, when I saw their faces for the first time, heard them cry, held them, and cried myself. In those moments I gained my clearest insights into selflessness. My daughters may not understand that unless or until they are parents, but they taught me what love is.

Down But Not Out

I was referred to Avide—a 36-year-old woman born in Iran— by the director of a women's shelter. Before Avide and I met, we talked on the phone about what would be involved in an interview, and whether she felt safe meeting with me. She actually seemed enthused about having a conversation. Later she sent me a text message and closed it, "Love, Avide." She used the same signature after a subsequent text message exchange.

I considered cancelling our interview, wondering if she was in any position emotionally to have the kind of conversation we'd end up having. We'd never met. She could not possibly love me. I struggled with whether or not to keep our appointment. In the end, I decided to keep it, and prepared myself for any number of potential scenarios that might unfold.

Avide was nothing like I had imagined. She was shy. Her expressions were muted. She spoke only in response to questions, in answers that were clipped. She was never able to take the conversation and carry it for even a short while.

I was grateful that I hadn't cancelled the interview, as I found her story profound. When I followed up with Avide a few days later to check in, she responded with a text message thanking me for the time together. She signed it with her customary, "Love, Avide." And it left me wondering whether she had anyone in her life to whom she could say, "I love you" and who says that to her.

Avide's text messages helped me understand the importance of those three words, how much we all want to touch someone else emotionally and be touched in return. It was the same lesson Luna, the sensual massage worker, left me with. They both helped me realize that wisdom and teachers come in all shapes and forms, not just the PhD types who'd been teaching me for years.

Avide was adopted by American parents after spending her first three years in an Iranian orphanage. Upon high school, she studied cosmetology. She worked as a hairdresser for several years, and then as a caregiver at an eldercare facility. After a period of homelessness, she was taking cleaning jobs when we met.

Avide told me that she did not know her adoptive father well. She had hazy notions of his family background and could only estimate his age at around 60 years old. "I think he went to college. My mom was a senior in high school and my dad was a couple years older when they met."

At some point, she said, her father served in the Marine Corps, though she did not know if he served in Vietnam, which would have been common for a former marine of his age. After his military discharge, he worked for AT&T, she said. "He would install their equipment in different states and he was always on the road. He was transferred with his job three times when I lived at home."

Avide's mother gave birth to three boys, but had always wanted girls. So instead of buying new living room furniture after she had saved for it, she decided to use the money instead to adopt daughters. She adopted Avide, who was three and a half, from Iran and a younger daughter from Honduras. Even with what she has gone through in life, Avide says she's glad she was adopted, because of the freedoms she has as an American.

Avide's earliest memories of her father are of him fighting with her mother. "You know how there's abuse, like domestic violence? Well, it was my mom that was abusing my dad, in a way. He was scared of her. And so he would just not talk much. He was real quiet, just gone a lot. She would be the one breaking stuff, throwing stuff at him. He would either leave the room or just stand there and take it."

Avide said that made her feel unsafe, as did abuse from both of her parents. "She was abusive to me, as well. She was not sexually abusive, but my dad was, from when I was in kindergarten all the way up until I was in my sophomore year in high school. It came out, because I would tell my sister and my sister knew. She never got sexually abused. My sister told the school, and the school had to report everything. We went to court and my mom had us lie in court that it didn't happen. She was scared that if he left, she would be homeless and she wouldn't have anything, because she was a housewife."

Her father has never apologized to her, she said. "He justifies it. He would say that because he wasn't getting it from his wife, that it was okay, instead of coming out and saying what he did was wrong. And that's one reason I don't have a relationship with him."

Avide had clear insights into how her parents' abuse shaped her, her view of men and of family life. "It was hard for me to trust people, and at the same time that's all I knew. I never knew what a healthy family would look like. When I met the guy that I would marry, because I had that abuse in the past, I thought it was normal. I would marry anybody just to get out of the house."

I asked about her beliefs and expectations of men. "The only thing I can think of is that if you got married to somebody, you'll be taken care of. In other words, the man will provide for you and you can be a housewife. So, just living at home, I always knew that the man would be the one that would provide. Men either have good careers or they're bums."

She learned as well that she could get men to meet some of her needs by appealing to them sexually. "I learned a lot, that I could use men in the beginning to get what I wanted. I was really promiscuous, dating different people just to have my needs met or get money.

I knew if I would sleep with them I could get anything I wanted. I knew that's what men like. Sex was what they wanted in life."

Avide said that at a deeper level, she was looking for intimacy and commitment from the men she was sexually involved with, but that it never came. "That's my heart's desire, to finally have somebody that is totally the opposite that I've ever experienced. And I know that if I'm going to have a man like that, he would have to be in my church, a godly man. He would have to believe in the Bible. Then he wouldn't be doing anything that's not right in God's eyes. Because I do believe there are Christian men out there that know how to treat a woman good. Somebody that I can trust, feel confident with, somebody that can pray with me and just lead as a man of the household."

She didn't find any of that in her first and only marriage. "We became homeless because my ex-husband wouldn't work. I left my job and took my son out of state for one month. When I came back, I was homeless. I went and stayed in a shelter. We were homeless for a couple of weeks before we moved into the transitional home. Now we're in an apartment.

"I had many chances to leave my husband, but I would always bring him back. If I had left him a lot earlier, I would have been able to raise my son full-time. The state realized that he had some stuff on the record, enough for them to tell me that it wasn't safe to be around him with my son. He hid a lot of stuff from me."

This young woman, and now single mother, grew up in an environment in which the man of the family could provide financial security but not safety—and in fact brought violence upon his daughter. Avide's self confidence and esteem were damaged by her early experience, and she became deeply depressed as an adult. "I fear that I won't be able to hold down a full-time job or be open with the next relationship. I pray that I will learn to deal with everything before that does happen, so I won't find myself in another abusive relationship.

"Right now, I'm learning to rely on God to help me with my basic needs. I started going to church this last summer and bringing my son. It's been helping us."

Avide has no relationship with her ex-husband or father now, and feels ongoing anger that she and her sister were forced to lie in court about her father's sexual abuse, and that as a result he didn't face any legal consequences.

As she told her story, it was clear that her father provided virtually nothing from the standpoint of being a healthy authority figure. "He never disciplined me. He never helped me with my homework. I don't believe he ever said anything important to me, anything that was wise or encouraging. I couldn't trust him one-on-one. But if I needed money for classes or I took ballet classes or extra activities at school, like volleyball, we were really secure financially."

Through counseling, Avide has begun piecing her life back together. "I learned that for one, it wasn't my fault. I would always take that blame. And I learned that who you're with has a big part of how you are as a person. In other words, if you're around somebody that's mean, ugly, you become like them."

Avide aspires to someday open her own hair salon, but she feels trapped by the fear that she's not good enough to do that kind of work, that she might fail at it, or make a mistake on someone's hair and make them mad. She told me, in a voice that was utterly serious, "If I was to mess up just even once, I'd probably quit the next day."

In spite of the anger that Avide grew up with and took into adulthood, she said she has forgiven her father. I asked her how she did that, and why. "Through the church, learning the word of God. In order to have that relationship with God, I would have to learn to forgive people, so God could forgive me as well for my sins. In other words, we're all sinners, even though one person's sin is different from somebody else's. I was taught in the Bible to forgive people and to have that peace. If I didn't want to let that anger control my life anymore, I would have to forgive him, but to know what he did was still wrong."

There was nothing uncertain in her voice when Avide claimed that she had forgiven her father. I mentioned that to her. "When my sister sees how I am, she goes, 'I don't know how you're doing it.' She hasn't forgiven my parents for some of the stuff that happened. And she can see that I can move on and that it's not eating me up, where it used to in the past. It wasn't until I went to counseling through the church and then when I got to be a member of the church that I could truly say I have forgiven him. Before then, I didn't even know God myself."

Through her counseling, Avide has made progress in her struggle with depression and authority issues that stem from the abuse she endured. "With my bosses, or people that were in leadership, or if I was doing volunteer work or anything, I could never have a good relationship with anybody. It'd always be a fight, even if they were my friends.

"Now, I'm starting to respect people and not have a big fight anytime I go out. It used to be where I couldn't go a day without having some kind of a confrontation with somebody or have any peace with anybody. But now, I can go somewhere and if there's a young girl that's a manager at a store, I'm not being evil to her just because she's younger than me. I can respect her now and treat her nicer, even if she's ahead of me in her career.

"Now I'm learning to rely on other people for help, if I need help, or if I need something I don't have to be scared to ask. My depression's gotten a lot better in that way. And I'm really involved with the church now, where we have things that we have to be at."

Even though she has forgiven her father, Avide decided to sever their relationship. "If I wanted that relationship, I could. But I just don't. He wants to be in his grandson's life. He wants the family times. And I have to do what's safe for me and my son. When I talked to him last, five years ago, he said he wanted all of that stuff. And I told him that it just can't happen."

I asked this woman what lesson she's learned from her hardships as a daughter that she could pass along to fathers. I was taken by how naturally she replied, how centered and grounded she was when she answered, how simple it was, yet how clear and profound.

"A relationship is really important and every child wants to have that with their father. No matter what job or stress they're going through, having good quality time is more important than making money and having the best stuff in the house, because that's just material stuff. The relationship is more important.

"I'd tell them to help their daughters with when they get into a relationship with a man. And if the father would bring the child to church or have some kind of relationship with God, that's important, as well. Also for the father to teach the daughter what to look forward to in a husband, so that way they will know what kind of person they would want to marry.

"And even if they don't like whatever hobbies the daughter has, he should find what her interests are or what her dreams are, to ask those questions before she moves out. Just the importance of having that relationship before they move out of the house, so she will be able to trust men in general."

Second Time
Is a Charm

My wife introduced me to Sheree a few months before we met for our interview. She has a son, who was four at the time. Sheree worked in the mortgage banking industry for fourteen years, then as a marketing vice president for a high tech start-up. More recently she has been working as a professional photographer.

Sheree's father was born in Southern California in 1937, the younger of two boys growing up in a family of alcoholism, infidelity, financial instability, divorce, and remarriage. That, as well as a childhood trauma, profoundly affected him.

"My dad had a pretty rough childhood in that his mother was a heavy partying woman. She wasn't a great mother. She would sit on the beach all the time to get a suntan and the kids would say, 'We wanna go home, we wanna go home.' She would send the kids to the movies all day and they would have to sit there. She would go to these military parties and leave her boys in the car. She was an alcoholic until she died. His step-father was an alcoholic, too. When my father was about ten years old, he was molested by another boy at the movie theater. And he never dealt with that.

"His dad wasn't an affectionate, loving kind of father. He adopted the children, but he was never a father figure emotionally. He provided really well and that's pretty much what my grandmother was looking for."

Sheree's father received an engineering degree from a university in the South, then moved back to Southern California where he met Sheree's mother. "My mom was eighteen and my dad was 25. She was engaged to be married, and the wedding was only about a week away. And then she met my dad. And it was, you know, love at first sight. My mom's parents owned this huge trailer park in Arizona, and they gave my parents a doublewide trailer to live in. Ten months later, I was born."

We talked about Sheree's early father-daughter memories and family folklore.

"Once when my great-grandmother was visiting, she saw me standing in the doorway of the bathroom, and my father was in there and I was pulling on his shirt, asking, 'Daddy, would you hold me, would you pick me up?' He pushed me away and said, 'I don't have time for you, I'm trying to do my hair.' He was very selfish, very into how he looked and really into himself. I could see that as I got older. It was all about him, what he wore, what kind of car he drove, even what kind of shoes he had on."

Sheree talked about how conflicted she was growing up—getting pieces of a normal family life from her father, and having him shatter it at the same time; wanting to be with a father, yet feeling hatred and resentment.

"My parents took us on very nice vacations. We had a second home up in Colorado. My father was a private pilot, so we would fly up there. He took me and my sister out. He would teach us how to play softball and other sports. And we always had Saint Bernards, so we would take the dogs out in the evening and walk them around. He would try to be engaged, in his way. Like we wanted to do a carnival one year for Muscular Dystrophy and raise money, so he helped us build a carnival in the back yard. And we had a huge tree on our property and he built a tree house. He taught us how to ski.

"But I disliked him so much that it was always a fight mentally for me. There was always a fight going on in my mind about, 'I hate you, I hate you, I hate you. But you're my father and I want to love you. But I hate you.' So I would want to do stuff with him, but then I wouldn't. I would just be thinking 'I *hate* you.' But I would never say that to him. I would just show it by not talking or just being grouchy or whatever.

"We had a lot of nice things, but I never recall a lot of one-on-one time. That was really okay because, as far back as I can remember, I never wanted to be close to him. He started abusing me sexually when I was about five years old. Anyway, there's a lot of hate towards him. And that's really the best word that I could say.

"I was saved as a child from not being crazy because I was able to be who I was and be a happy person and put my home life to the side when I went to school. When I was in the fifth grade, they sent us to a private Christian school. My parents were both Christians and we attended church for my whole life. That rubbed me the wrong way for a long time; how could my father be such a hypocrite? But it didn't harden my heart. God gave me a soft heart. So that was good, because I had friends at school and that was the place where I could just be me. That really saved me as a person."

Sheree said her father abused her about once a week, usually after he'd been drinking. "I would always pretend to be asleep. There was never any penetration or anything like that, just touching. And when he was confronted with it years later, he said, 'Oh, I always thought you were asleep. If I'd known you weren't asleep, I wouldn't have done it.' And I thought, 'Like it should make a difference if I was awake or asleep?'

"My mom didn't know. And it's the standard thing that every victim says: You never want to say anything because you're so afraid of tearing the family apart. I was so afraid that I would be the one that caused my parents to divorce. As much as I couldn't stand my dad, I didn't want to be the cause of the family breaking up.

"So I dealt with it by being a really angry child. My mom would always say, 'We don't understand why she's such a crabby kid. She's always got a chip on her shoulder about something.' And they'd go in for parent-teacher conferences and the teachers would say, 'Our biggest problem with Sheree is she talks so much and she's so social,' and my parents would say, 'You sure we're talking about the same kid? Because we don't see that. She's always in her room and she's always quiet, not a very happy child.'

"I loved my school and my friends. That was the place for me to develop as a child and as a person. I had wonderful teachers. And I think some of them were father figures for me. They cared about me in a very healthy, normal way. That was really good for me.

"As a woman of faith, I think that God provided those people in my life to help me move forward without becoming a completely wrecked person. I always felt that I didn't want to be a victim my whole life. That just wasn't my deal. I wanted to move on. It sucked and it was horrible and I hated it, and now as I go to counseling, I learn some of the emotional damage it caused me, and the emotional baggage I have and I have to deal with."

Sheree was able to calmly talk about what she took from that relationship. "I really struggle a lot with getting in touch with and showing my emotions. I guess I shoved them all away in an intimate setting for such a long period of time that that's the pattern I developed. My husband shows more emotion than I do. Our counselor is helping me learn how to get more in touch with my emotions like sadness and more feminine emotions. Because I chose to be strong, like, 'I'm not gonna be a victim. I'm just gonna deal with it and I'm gonna not succumb to this asshole. I'm just not going to.'

"Sometimes that's how I want my son to be, to be strong. I don't want him to cry, like when he falls down or something, I want to be compassionate but I'm like, 'No, it's okay, get up, you're all right, let's go.' And my husband taught me, 'Sometimes you have to just give him a hug and a kiss and let him know it's okay.' And I didn't even know that."

I thought Sheree's story about her father being too busy with his hair to pick her up and hold her was a metaphor for their life together. Like any daughter, she wanted her father's attention and love, to feel him holding her. And instead of providing that safety, security, and affection he lived a life of self-indulgence.

"It was hard. But you know, when you don't know any different, which I didn't, it was just survival. He wanted to control everything. My mother had absolutely no say about anything. He molded her personality because they got married so young."

Sheree told a story to illustrate her mother's timidity. The incident took place after Sheree's sophomore year in high school. "My mother was trying to make a decision about something and it was such a miniscule kind of a decision, and she couldn't make it. I said to her, 'You know, Mom, I never ever, ever want to have a relationship like you have because you need Dad to make every decision that you ever make for yourself.' I couldn't believe I said that to her. And she later told me she's never forgotten that. That was very big for me. I was the timid person when it came to my family. I never said anything."

Sheree's inhibition grew out of her fear of domination and punishment. "We were disciplined through fear, fear of him, fear of the belt. I don't necessarily think that spanking is incorrect, but the way it was done in my family it was totally misused. There was never a specific reason; it was never explained to you why you were being punished. It was almost a form of abuse."

Her father's sexual abuse continued until Sheree was sixteen. It came to light as the family was fraying, shortly after they had moved to California. Sheree's parents were having a heated argument one night, so she and her fourteen-year-old sister left home and checked into a motel to escape the fighting.

"We stayed up the whole night and talked, and I told her what had been happening to me. And she said it happened for a really short period to her, and she had said something to Mom and Mom was like, 'Oh, honey, I'm sure it's nothing.' And so Mom had said something to Dad about it, something like, 'She was complaining that you come in and tuck her in at night and she doesn't really like that.' And so it stopped. My sister said, 'I can't believe he's still doing it to you.' So the next day my sister told my mom. That was the beginning of the end of their marriage.

"And you know what? At that point, I was perfectly fine with my mother not being married to my father any more. I had no guilt about it. I didn't feel like it was my fault, I didn't feel like it was gonna be a burden that I would carry. To this day I have no guilt about it at all. It practically put my mother in the grave, that she didn't know, that it went on, and it was her child. How could he do that to his own flesh and blood? She never, ever, ever made me feel bad about not coming to tell her. My father never denied it."

In a turning point for her, Sheree's mother mustered the courage to confront her husband. He apologized repeatedly, and even came to counseling once with Sheree and apologized there as well. But as far as Sheree was concerned, her father was in the past.

"It didn't really mean anything to me, and it still doesn't mean anything to me. It's not worth it to me to spend a lot of wasted energy disliking an individual. I don't hate him. I've forgiven him for what he's done. But because I've forgiven him, that doesn't mean I have to like him. I don't necessarily care for him as a person, so I choose not to have a relationship with him, and I would never trust him with my child. So instead of having to deal with him and saying, 'I don't want you to be around my child,' it's just easier for me just not to have a relationship with him. So I don't. And I haven't since I was 29 years old. And I've had complete peace about it."

The trauma of abuse puts a profound imprint on the minds of daughters such as Sheree. The unconscious beliefs that get laid down during those years shape a girl's sense of herself, her desirability, and her ability to form and sustain intimate, trusting relationships. Unraveling the damage takes an extraordinary amount of work, and there's usually tremendous hardship along the way, as Sheree found out.

"I did the hard-core therapy a while back, sixteen, seventeen years ago. And I've gone back recently. I was married before, and my husband left me when I went to therapy. I didn't feel safe to go to therapy until I was married. So when I got married at 25, I started therapy after we'd been married about six months. I knew that at some point in my life I had to deal with the sexual abuse.

"I knew because it was such a long period of my childhood, that it was such a big part of my life, I had to do something. I was living in LA and my mom said, 'You're in LA, there's got to be a lot of really good therapists that specialize in that. If you're willing to go, I'm going to have your father pay for it.' So he paid for all of it.

"We found a woman who specialized in working with adults who'd had child sexual abuse. And she was really great. I did individual therapy for about three years, and then I did group therapy for about two years. Now that I'm married again, and doing therapy as a married woman, I've learned more about peeling the layers away and learning more about myself in a relationship. The biggest thing I've learned as an adult is how as a survivor of sexual abuse, it's very hard for me to get in touch with my emotions. I didn't learn that when I was in therapy in my twenties. Back then I was just more dealing with the trauma. Now I'm learning about the really relevant part of everyday living, and what I lost as a child.

"Before I got married the second time, I saw a therapist on and off because I could never understand why I couldn't pick people that could make a commitment. I probably attracted the same kind of people that I was. They probably weren't ready to be committed emotionally. And even though I thought I was, I probably put out vibes that I wasn't emotionally ready to make a commitment.

"So nobody I dated ever wanted to make a commitment, because they probably thought I wasn't ready to either," she laughed. "Oh, that's so funny! I never thought of it that way. And then when I would meet one guy in particular who was pretty needy and ready to be in a relationship, I wanted nothing to do with it."

While the damage her father inflicted was profound, Sheree had other men in her life who offered some counterweight to her father's selfishness. "I don't hate men today, which is probably kind of strange. I did have other role models in my life, like some of the teachers that I mentioned. They were great men, so I knew men weren't all bad.

"My mom remarried when I was about eighteen, and I wasn't really happy about it. I wanted Mom to stay single. But then I got to know her husband, and I thoroughly enjoyed him. I moved in with them for about a year after my divorce, while I was going through therapy. That's when I really got to know Grant, and the compassionate, fatherly side of who he was. And that's when I fell in love with him as a dad. He kind of plugged the holes of all those emotional needs of a father that I had.

"I kind of felt whole, like 'Wow, this is like having a dad! This is like having a mom and a dad and I can sleep at night. I can feel this is a safe place to be.' That was really a big one for me: a safe place to be. I can come home and I can sleep at night and not wonder who's going to come in my room.

"Grant was really gifted in the therapy side of life. He was a real estate appraiser and I worked for him during that time when I lived with them. He taught me how to do appraisals, which added another aspect to my career. During the time that I worked for him, he shared so many things with me about being married and trust and relationships, and everything a dad would say to someone that age. It was just unbelievable to me to have somebody like that, that you can trust, you can love, that loves you and it's unconditional. It made me feel whole.

"He passed away last May, of early onset Alzheimer's. The last few years of his life, I helped Mom care for him. He had to go into a home the last year of his life, so I would visit him every day, and try to be there for lunch time and feed him and make sure he was okay. That was a really hard time, and a very sorrowful loss. Sometimes I just can't believe that he's gone." Sheree began crying. "I just can't believe it. On every card I sent him, I would always write that God brought him to our family, that he was our gift from God. He really, really was."

The Resurrection

Katie was my sixth-grade sweetheart, whom I wrote about in my introduction. We found each other on a classmates web site in our mid-forties. She was living in San Diego. I told her that if my travels took me there, I would let her know. About a year later, while I was on a business trip, we met at the airport.

Katie showed up, semi-coherent, under the influence of God-knows-what. We sat in an airport restaurant and talked for hours. She'd been through five marriages, three suicide attempts and countless doctors who—ignorant of her addiction—piled drug prescriptions on top of each other. Unable to parent, she'd left her children with their father and moved out of state.

In my early fifties, as I was recruiting women to interview for this book, I suspected Katie had an important father-daughter story. I sent her an email asking if she would be willing to talk with me. She replied: "I am the wrong person for your book. My dad had nothing to do with who I am. Life did. I grew up without a dad. No...I am not pissed off...although it does sound like it with my reply."

Six months later Katie was living with her father and mother. She had gained the ability to see that she did have a father and that he had shaped her. In a subsequent email she wrote, "You know, I really believe that my bad luck with men stems from my relationship with my father. Although our relationship is better, it is still strained to some degree. As a grown woman in her fifties, there is still a little girl inside of me who is waiting for her knight in shining armor. I still long for the father I never had. Although these feelings are manageable now, they continue to haunt me."

Eight months later, Katie agreed to meet with me for an interview. Hers is a story of near death and redemption.

By the time we sat down to talk Katie had stopped drinking, smoking, and mixing drug cocktails. She was making jewelry and doing artistic work. "I can take anybody's junk and find some beauty in it, make something out of it," she said.

"My life was just a party. I didn't want to deal with anything serious. I was like tumbleweed, just blowing in the wind. Wherever it stopped, I would stop and if the wind picked up, I was gone again. And I'd use any chemical that could keep me from thinking too much about what I should have been thinking about and doing to get my head screwed on. All through my twenties I traveled and partied and made money and pissed it away, never saved a dime. I just had so much self-hate and horrible self-esteem."

Katie's first marriage was at nineteen, to a man she soon discovered was gay. She married again at 28, to the father of her one-year-old child, in a relationship centered around parties and drugs. She remarried several times after that.

Katie tried to kill herself three times. The first time she slit her wrists. The last attempt was in 2001, when she consumed a bottle of Tylenol and nearly two bottles of wine. She went into cardiac arrest and was in a coma for three days.

During her coma Katie had an out of body experience and a communion with God. "That's when everything turned around for me, because I didn't see Him, but I knew there was a presence and I was somewhere I've never been before in this life. It's not of this life. It was something completely different.

"I just clearly remember feeling or hearing this—it wasn't a voice. It was a very large thought, but it wasn't mine, that said, 'You have something very large to do. And you have to stay around to get it done. You're just not going anywhere.'" That experience put her on a path of redemption with her father, who had abused her as a child.

Born in Michigan, he was raised on a farm by an overbearing mother, "a tyrant," Katie said, whom he resented. At eighteen he joined the Air Force, and then got married.

"He's been a piece of work and was a big thorn in my side all my life," Katie said. "Some woman who worked with him filed a sexual harassment lawsuit against him. My earliest memory of him was he was a womanizer and an abuser. He abused my mother and he abused his kids.

"The belt was always out. He would use the belt buckle side on my brothers and I would have to take care of their butt cheeks because there were holes in them from the buckle, he beat them so bad. And he beat me, too. He slapped me around a lot, one time so hard that I hit the corner of a wall and cracked my head open. And he had to take me to the hospital. I had to get some stitches in my head.

"I remember when he brought me home. I didn't have a fever, but he insisted on taking my temperature with a rectal thermometer, and having sex with that thermometer in my ass. And my mother had come in the room and said, 'What are you doing to her? She doesn't have a fever.' I had blood coming out of my anus for a week after that and I never told my mother. I hated him. I really did hate him. Everything he did I just knew was wrong and evil.

"When I was a teenager, I was very rebellious and ran away a lot, abused a lot of street drugs, drank a lot, was sexually promiscuous, because I thought that was how I was going to get love, because that's how my father was. My father was constantly making remarks about women's anatomy and smacking my mother around and treating my mother and I like second class citizens. Everything I did was wrong, not good enough."

What was Katie taking in from her father? That women were sex objects; that she was worthless. Yet Katie's story demonstrates how father-daughter relationships do not end when the daughter leaves home. Parenting never ends; and sometimes it's the child who parents her mother or father. Katie's story is also a testament to the power of forgiveness.

After her last suicide attempt, and the spiritual experience that came with it, Katie put herself into therapy. One by one, she vanquished her demons: cigarettes, booze, Valium, Xanax, Vicodin, Percoset. Katie had promised her mother years before that if she ever needed help, she would be there. And when her mother had serious health problems, Katie moved to the Nevada desert to live with her parents for a month.

By then, Katie was a different woman. She was taking long walks. She would spend days alone in the desert, listening to her inner spirit.

"Making the desert road trips, I found big therapy there. I would just get these very strong thoughts. They didn't seem like my own. They were coming from somewhere. Without any commotion going on around me, all kinds of stuff comes to me. It's like every wall in me is gone and I'm really receptive to all these insights. That's where I really grew by leaps and bounds personally. I became more aware of me and what I wanted to do and who I really am, and my parents were seeing that.

"From 51 until 53, that's when our relationship was repaired, because I was repaired. I had gotten through all my issues. Well, I realized once I was there, I didn't want to go back to San Diego, so I asked if I could stay. I was helping my father, but I didn't know it. I got him to try to see life sober, to see the beauty in things around him, to get in touch with himself and his feelings and his past, to let go of the anger he had with his own mother and his brother, even though they're dead.

"I remember him saying, 'What are you doing, because you seem lighter; you seem happier; you seem freer; something's different.' I told him it was the road trips into the desert. You go out there and park and listen to nothing and you're going to hear something; you're going to hear a lot. You can't run from yourself anymore when there's nowhere to go and you're stuck with no human contact.

"And he saw me working with my art, my painting, my jewelry, the things I made. He got to know how I think and how I feel. He would hear my phone calls with my kids. We lived together as adults without the bullshit when I was younger. So we were both really seeing the other person the way we are now.

"We both grew in that two and a half years and our relationship benefited from it immensely. I'm not mad at him anymore. I forgive him for all of it. He was a very sick man and he didn't know how to ask for help. So he hurt the ones closest to him. It wasn't until the last two and a half years I lived with him that he finally saw me as me and accepted me and he's blown away by who I am. And so in the last two and a half years I've gotten more pats on the back from him than I did in my whole life."

As Katie spoke, I had no doubt about the conviction and authenticity of that forgiveness. But I simply couldn't comprehend how she had gotten to such a point. So I asked her where in the universe she found the grace to forgive her father and let go of the anger. Like several of the other women I spoke with, she said she knew it was the only way she could heal herself.

"You have to forgive, because if you don't, it festers inside of you like cancer. You may think you're not thinking about it, but it's always there and it eats at you. I knew in order to get past it, to get to the next level, I had to sincerely forgive my father. And because I have, that opened up so many doors for me. And I'm able to love completely now, holding nothing back, expecting nothing from anybody. I just love so unconditionally. It's freed me.

"It took two years for me to realize the man loves me. He always loved me. He just didn't have the right tools to show me and he didn't have the tools to be a good parent, because he had his own issues. Now when we're together, we have a great time. And he's so happy for me and he's so happy how I've turned out. He got to learn a lot about me, what I'd been through, not just my childhood that he's probably forgot, but my relationships. And he learned things that happened to me that he didn't know about. So, it's almost as if he's at peace now and he's let go of his issues and forgiven himself."

For the first time in his life, he told Katie he loved her when she was 52. When I asked her what that was like, she said, "I about fell over. I actually stopped what I was doing and turned around and said, 'What?' He said, 'I love you. I think you should know that.' And he would say it more and then, I found that I was saying back, 'I love you, too,' instead of just going, 'Oh, okay.'"

I asked Katie what was happening the first time her father said he loved her, because I had a hunch. I was right. She said he was crying. "He's had regrets and I've told him that I've forgiven him. I'm like, 'I accept your apology. I don't want you to spend the last years of your life kicking yourself in the butt for stuff that's happened. Just know I love you and I forgive you for it.'

"I cried with him. It choked me up, because I didn't think he had any sensitivity in him at all. I thought he was just a hard-nosed jerk. But he's a real soft man. I think the years of abuse that he did to himself and the way his mother treated him, he just didn't know how to get off that."

I reminded Katie of how she had started our conversation by saying, "I can take anybody's junk and make something beautiful out of it." I told her that was a metaphor for her life, that she took her father's discarded daughter and made a beautiful life.

"I never looked at it that way," she said. "That's so true, because it could have gone the other way so easily. Wow. Thank you."

I contacted Katie a few days after our interview, as I did with most of the women I'd met. These conversations stirred an emotional pot, particularly for those women who drew the short straw with their fathers. So I always wanted to know if they felt unsettled, and several times I offered referrals to therapists who I thought might be helpful.

In introducing her story, I shared two emails she had sent me, the first being her declaration that her father had nothing to do with who she'd become. In her second email, she was awakening to the role her father had played in her troubled relationships with men, and how she had spent much of her life looking for her "knight in shining armor." This was Katie's email reply after our interview:

"I slept like a rock. The only difference was my dreams. They were all about forgiveness and letting go of past hurts. Pretty amazing stuff. I want you to know something. I have always known I have forgiven my father. But yesterday when we were talking, or I was, reliving all that crap, was confirmation that I have truly forgiven him.

"It did not affect me in a negative way at all. It's as if I received validation for my forgiveness. I never loved my father until I spent time with him in the desert and got to know him as an adult. I am truly grateful I have him now rather than never having him and holding on to the anger and resentment that followed me all my life. How stifling it was for me and him also."

Conclusion

> This body is as transient as dew on the grass.
> Life passes as swiftly as a flash of lightening.
> Quickly the body passes away,
> In a moment life is gone.
>
> Great Zen Master Dogen
> 12th century

Time is short, I thought, when I started to question myself as a father. It was exactly two years ago as I write this, in the days between Christmas and the New Year. That's when I began wondering what it's like to be the daughter of a father. How was I shaping my daughters without even thinking about it, I wondered? What do I have left to teach them?

The past two years have been an emotional roller coaster. I left the corporate world and started my own business. I found a new life. I found my daughters.

Among the numerous wakeup calls that I got over the past two years was an announcement from my older daughter Julia in the summer of 2010. After one year of high school, and a month shy of her fifteenth birthday, she declared that she wanted to begin college. She found an early entry program at a private college in Virginia and applied for admission in June.

The whole thing unfolded in a blur. We did a family interview by telephone. She was accepted in July. I bought plane tickets in August, and before the end of the month we were gone.

239

Buying our tickets as late as we did meant we took three flights, including a red-eye, and then drove 90 miles to the college. I was sick with the stomach flu and hadn't been able to eat for three days. My wife had offered to take my place, but I wanted to do this. This was my job.

I felt an enormous loss as I flew with her across the country. As the first flight was rolling down the runway for takeoff, Julia reached over and held my hand.

I wanted to make sure she knew how to navigate her way through airports, so I asked her to show me what we needed to do at each step along the way once we were on our first flight. Where do we go? What do we do next? What would we do if we needed help? She had it all figured out.

Our trip took about sixteen hours, including layovers and the drive time after we landed. I was too sick, and she was too tired, to really talk much. We arrived at the college about noon, exhausted, having not slept all night. There was an orientation a few hours later. I collapsed on a bare mattress in a spare dorm room, hoping to get a few hours of sleep.

After the orientation we dragged ourselves to the dining hall for our last dinner together. It felt a bit like a proverbial last supper, an end to the life I'd known and spent with my daughter of barely fifteen years. Surprisingly, we didn't see any other parents there when we arrived. After a few minutes, Julia looked around and said, "Dad, I'm the only one here not sitting with any other girls."

"Do you want to go sit somewhere else?" I asked.

"I think so," she replied.

So she got up, walked to a nearby table and joined six older girls. Within ten minutes she was part of the pack.

I felt alone, but that feeling passed as I realized it was the healthiest thing she could have done.

About an hour later, I told Julia I had to leave, so I could drive back to my hotel before it got dark. "I'm not ready for you to go yet," she said. The tenderness of that moment touched my heart. I knew it was probably the last time she would ever say to me, "I'm not ready for you to go yet." I stayed for another 45 minutes. And then, finally, I did have to leave. It wasn't easy. Julia was excited but nervous. I just felt empty.

Coming home was a struggle. As I flew back across the country, I remembered our morning ritual as I left for work when she was four or five. Julia would run to the front door shouting, "You can't leave without a hug and kiss!" So we would give each other a hug and kiss.

As the years went by, the departure ritual simplified. Soon she only needed to see me from the top of the stairs and say, "Huggy kiss," as she blew me a kiss. Then, for perhaps another year, she would simply shout, "Huggy kiss!" from wherever she was, not needing to make any visual connection. That, in time, evolved simply into a shout of, "Bye, Dad." Before I knew it, I was sometimes leaving for work or she was leaving for school without saying good-bye at all.

I felt I'd lost my race against time. Thirteen years earlier I had a two-year-old daughter and she cried, "I want my daddy back." As I replayed the memories during my flight home, my heart just sank. Where did she go? I wanted a do-over. There was too much left that I hadn't done. I wanted my daughter back. And it was too late.

It was not too late for my younger daughter Kat, who had just turned eleven. Two days after I got back from taking Julia to college, I flew to San Francisco with Kat, just as I'd done with Julia when she was eleven. We rented a car and took a week-long road trip up the California and Oregon coasts, just the two of us. We went body surfing in Santa Cruz and braved the boardwalk rides. We went to Fisherman's Wharf and rode cable cars in San Francisco. We drove through the Redwood Forest, then up the Oregon coast. We stayed in hotels along the way and she thought those were cool.

Kids absorb their parents' influence in many ways. Sometimes it's through trauma, such as abandonment or abuse. That's what early psychoanalytic thinkers focused on. Over time psychologists came to appreciate how we're shaped by the everyday routines of our environments.

Our parents hold countless beliefs, most of them unconscious. "The world is dangerous." Or, "Work is something you do at a company." Or, "Men need to support their families." Or, "Getting drunk isn't a big deal." Beliefs guide parents' behavior, which in turn forms the family culture. Children internalize much of that culture, and those beliefs get implanted in their minds without any fanfare. Sometimes we recognize those beliefs, and sometimes we don't. Many remain unconscious and put our lives on an autopilot. The lucky among us get help digging through those old tapes, and how they govern our perceptions, feelings, and behavior.

Kids learn what they see. Everything communicates. Recall the daughters of broken marriages—such as Luna and Leilani—who shared their beliefs about marriage not being sustainable. That fragility was their world as their young minds were being molded; that's what they know. Or rather, that's what they believe to be true. For women like Cheryl Coupé and Ruth Burk, marriage is the great experience you get to have for a lifetime with your best friend.

These women live in the same world. They're the same age. They all have access to the same data about marriage and divorce. They simply see the world differently, as we all do, based upon our early conditioning. What we believe shapes what we selectively perceive, and that in turn reinforces what we believe. It's a vicious cycle, and fathers have a lot to do with how our cycles get started.

We have all kinds of things we want to teach our daughters, such as responsibility, cooperation, respect. Most of what we teach, though, simply comes from how we live and the examples we set. That hit me in the gut as I sat with these women and heard their stories. Each was a mirror held up for me. I saw the shadows of my successes and heard the echo of my failures in their lives with their fathers. What I learned in these sessions was intensely personal. The hardest lesson was watching my blind spots come into plain view, and realizing how much I didn't know.

The flip side of course is that I feel enormous gratitude for what I learned. The awareness I gained from my conversations changed how I parent in ways that were immediate. I played more. I tried to work a little less. I became more sensitive. And I found it became a lot easier to question my knee-jerk responses to things in my family.

For example, during this work I was searching web sites for a particularly used car I wanted. I found it in Fremont, California. When I told my wife I was going to fly down and drive the car home, she suggested I take Julia. After initially tripping over the $200 for another plane ticket, I realized I'd never again get to drive my 13-year-old daughter up Interstate 5 with the top down in a little red convertible. A few days later, we were bombing north through the central California valley and around Mount Shasta with the sun beating down on us and the wind blowing through our hair.

Another time, I had to hang a hose rack on the back wall of our house. So I asked Kat if she wanted to learn how to use a power drill. Of course she did. She'd never bored holes into the outside wall of a house; that was almost as fun for a kid as blowing things up (well, for my kids anyway). So what would have been just another chore for me a year earlier became instead something fun that we did together: "That was awesome," she said, after blasting into the wood.

Small things like these were among the stepping stones on my journey of awakening. My teachers along the way have been remarkable. I was touched by the profound wisdom of ordinary women and fathers. I didn't make a point of interviewing academic scholars, experts, or geniuses. Genius is right in front of us, everywhere.

I'm asked all the time if I can distill what I learned along my journey. Yes, I can. I've put those lessons into the following letter. It's from every newborn daughter to her father. It's also a video on YouTube, featuring daughters that I've come to know.

Dear Dad,

After nine months in the dark, I have just spent 21 hours fighting my way out of that warm, cramped space. I was so happy to see you that I burst out crying.

I already know your voice. And I already feel an attachment to you. Please, don't ever leave me. Hold me, hug me, and love me every day. Let me sleep on your chest and feel the rhythm of your life feed mine.

I need to be with you. I want you to want me with you. Tell me you love me. Show me you love me. Take me places and do things with me, just me. Anything you want to do is fine. We can go to the race track or parades or baseball games. We can go to breakfast or movies together. We can play catch outside. Take me with you in your garbage truck or to your office.

Take me camping, even if it's just in our back yard. I need someone to treasure me and fill my heart. If you don't do it, I may spend the rest of my life looking for someone who will.

Swing me high in the air above your head at the beach. Give me piggyback rides. Chase me and catch me and tickle me. Swim like a shark under water and capture me, then throw me into the air. Let me crawl into bed between you and Mom and then hug me some more. Let me see you smile.

Read to me. Tell me stories. You can make them up, any kind of stories. Tell me about when you were a little boy. Tuck me into bed at night. Let me talk to you, and listen to me, really listen. Try to hear what's in my heart, because I won't always know for sure.

Teach me how to be strong and fierce and how to fight for myself. Lay down the law and hold me to it, even when I whine. Show me how to work hard. Teach me about money and power and how to navigate in the world.

Love Mom forever. Show me what I should look for in a life partner by the example you set. Show me I deserve someone who will cherish me, have fun with me, listen to me, bring me flowers for no reason at all. Be the sort of husband that you'd want me to have.

Take me to church, to temple, to God. Help me find the Big Spirit and reverence inside myself, other people, and everything else.

Hold my hand and hug me, even as I get older. Tell me I'm beautiful. Let me hear what it feels like when it comes from someone who loves me.

Tell me about yourself. Open your heart to me. Let me know who you really are. Help me come to know you as a man, not just as Planet Dad circling around me as I spin at the center of my own chaotic universe.

Hold me to the high standard of the woman I'll be grateful to become. Whoever I meet and date, hold them to a high standard, too. Be firm. I don't need a friend. I need a Father.

Accept and love me for who I am. I may not be the daughter you fantasized about. There may be an artist inside of me, not a doctor. There may be an engineer inside me, not a writer. I may have women lovers, not men. I may choose another religion or none at all. I will find my own political beliefs. Help me find myself. Encourage me. Love me unconditionally, even as I'm different. Just like you were.

Please, Daddy, find yourself. Don't live a miserable life. Don't do it for me. Don't do it for anyone. Let me see love in your heart and light in your soul.

Let me go when my time has come. But the best place you can be is around the corner□out of sight, yet close enough that if I ever need you, you will be there.

Take care of yourself, too. I want my children to know you. I want them to know why I'm crying so hard when I bury you, just like I cried when I came into this world.

Love,
Your Daughter

Epilogue

When I took Julia to Virginia, I knew it would be hard for her to be uprooted from everyone and everything she knew and dropped into a small, southern women's college. So did she.

Over the following weeks, she came to realize that it wasn't the experience she'd hoped for. She said that she'd made a mistake; that if she had only four years to spend at college she'd better spend them someplace where she was happier, someplace that fit her better. She said she wanted to come back home and to high school. She withdrew from her classes and posted a good-bye letter on Facebook:

```
Dear Virginia,

    I know this will be hard, but I believe it would
be best if we broke up. Our political views, our
goals in life, and our ideas of independence (I'm be-
ginning to feel stifled by our relationship) are so
different that I don't feel we could ever be happy.
I've also realized that I have feelings for my ex,
Portland, who I'll be moving back in with this week-
end. I hope we can still be friends.

    Love, Julia.
```

249

The father-daughter relationship I had laid to rest came back from the burial I'd given it. A few weeks earlier, as I flew back from Virginia, I wanted my daughter back and I wanted a do-over. Now I have my second chance with her, and with my daughter Kat as well.

When I started the interviews for this book, I had a nagging question among the many swirling through my mind during that snowstorm: What do I have left to teach my daughters in the short time we have left together? I got an important answer. It's that my task was as much about what I had to learn—and from daughters, no less—as what I had teach my girls.

I discovered that by allowing myself to be raised by a global tribe of adult daughters—young and old, rich and poor, famous and anonymous—I was creating a new blueprint for myself as a father. I hope it creates one for other fathers as well, around the world. If more men would listen to the stories within the hearts and souls of the women, and really hear them, the world would be a better place. There would be a lot fewer women dropped on the doorstep of young adulthood neglected, discarded, and damaged by the men who are supposed to guide them there.

The conversations that led to this book forever changed my life. My frantically busy mind has slowed a bit. I take more time to do what I like, such as writing this book, exercising, and hanging out with my daughters. I'll make money sometime later. Or maybe I won't. Today, I have more important work to do.

Acknowledgements

I am deeply grateful to the many people who helped make this book possible. These include Bernadette Zavala, MPH; Betsy Davenport, PhD; Kate Kavanagh, Ph.D., Catherine Paglin, PhD; Cheryl Coupé, MFA; Diana Page Jordan; Elissa Tomasini; John Flanagan, LCSW; Kerry McClenahan; Priscilla Ditewig; Robert Stuckey, PhD; and Steve Woodward, MA.

Thank you to all the women who had the courage and trust to share their lives with me. In the editing of this book, not all of their stories could be included, but what they shared with me contributed to my thinking and final presentation. Those whose stories are not included are:

Ann Schneider, United States
Barbara Wilson, United States
Becky Alderin, United States
Betty Beard, United States
Betty Roberts, United States
Christina Renck, Germany
Denise Erickson, United States
Erika Robles-Jones, Mexico
Jane Kim, Korea
Joie Smith, United States
Laura Mahoney, United States
Linda Knudson, United States
Meg DesCamp, United States
Majvor Cherkauer, Finland
Nancy Wells, United States
Patricia Risley, United States

Tammie Coelho, United States
Tess Morgan, United States
Tine Thissen, The Netherlands
Finally, thank you to my wife, Meg DesCamp, for her commitment to parenting and for assisting with everything from transcription to editing on this project.

Author Bio

A former journalist, Kevin Renner holds an undergraduate degree in social sciences with honors from the University of California at Santa Cruz. He later earned his Masters of Business Administration from the University of California at Berkeley. While there, he lived in a large global community of students and scholars at the International House. As a marketing executive, his work has taken him throughout the U.S., Europe, and Asia.

As the founder and president of B2B Market Strategies, Kevin divides his time among his family, writing, and his work as a marketing and brand strategist to emerging companies. He lives in Portland, Oregon with his wife Meg, daughters Katherine and Julia, and an ever-evolving animal population.

In the months since his book's release, Renner has appeared on NPR, CBS, NBC, Fox, ABC, and the Oprah Winfrey radio and television affiliates around the country. He writes and speaks now on fathers and daughters.

http://kevin-renner.com/ ♥ http://twitter.com/KevinRenner
http://www.facebook.com/pages/
Kevin-Renner-In-Search-of-Fatherhood/176384809075969

More Praise for
In Search of Fatherhood

This is not a book you "can't put down." You will need and will want to put it down -- to ponder and let the lessons sink in. You will need to catch your breath and appreciate the pure joy in the stories of wonderful father/daughter relationships as well as to marvel at the daughters who triumphed in the face of horrific relationships with their fathers. It is clear that writing this book changed the author's life. There is a good chance it will do the same for its readers.

Kenton R. Hill, Ed.D., author of
Smart Isn't Enough: How Developing Your Emotional Intelligence Can Transform Your Life and Career

The interviews are often touching in their emotional rawness and the crystalline clarity with which many women – decades removed from their childhood – recall poignant moments with their fathers. As the book makes clear, it's the small, special moments in daily life, rather than the grand, dramatic gestures, that seem to stick.

James Broderick, PhD, New Jersey City University

Paraphrasing Esther Perel (*Mating in Captivity*) who has said: "Tell me how you were loved, and I'll tell you how you make love," reading Kevin Renner's memoir of fatherhood prompts me to say to women, regardless of age, culture, or background: "Tell me if and how your father loved you as a child, and I'll tell you whether or not you have found love as a woman."

Charlene Kate Kavanagh, Ph.D., psychologist and author